EARLY CHILDHOOD EDUCATION SERIES

Leslie R. Williams, Editor

Millie Almy, Senior Advisor

ADVISORY BOARD: Barbara T. Bowman, Harriet K. Cuffaro,
Doris Pronin Fromberg, Celia Genishi, Alice Sterling Honig,
Elizabeth Jones, Gwen Morgan, David Weikart

Professionalism
and the
Early Childhood Practitioner

Bernard Spodek
Olivia N. Saracho
Donald L. Peters
EDITORS

Teachers College • Columbia University
New York and London

Published by Teachers College Press, 1234 Amsterdam Avenue,
New York, NY 10027

Library of Congress Cataloging-in-Publication Data

Professionalism and the early childhood practitioner.
  (Early childhood education series)
  Bibliography: p.
  Includes index.
  1. Early childhood education—Vocational guidance
—United States.   2. Preschool teachers—Training of—
United States.   I. Spodek, Bernard.   II. Saracho,
Olivia N.   III. Peters, Donald L.   IV. Series.
LB1775.5.P76   1988   372'.21   87-33643
ISBN 0-8077-2896-9
ISBN 0-8077-2895-0 (pbk.)

Manufactured in the United States of America

93 92 91 90 89 88   1 2 3 4 5 6

Contents

PART III   TOWARD DEVELOPING
PROFESSIONALISM

Part I

FOUNDATIONS
OF PROFESSIONALISM

1 • Professionalism, Semiprofessionalism, and Craftsmanship

BERNARD SPODEK
University of Illinois

OLIVIA N. SARACHO
University of Maryland

DONALD L. PETERS
University of Delaware

Early childhood programs have a history of at least 150 years' duration in the United States. That history has been unbroken since the establishment of English-language kindergartens in the 1860s and their slow assimilation into the public schools beginning in the 1870s. It has influenced everything from the labeling of those employed to the expectations held for their performance by the general public. It is not truly a single history, but rather several histories. The evolution of the early childhood field is that of several movements—the kindergarten movement, the nursery school movement, the day-care movement, and, more recently, the early intervention or compensatory education movement—each with its own history and its own development. That these movements continue to have a separateness and have yet to come together under one conception of early childhood education is central to understanding the debate surrounding issues of professionalism.

ESTABLISHING EARLY CHILDHOOD PRACTICE

Early childhood education practitioners a century ago were not called *teachers*, but rather *kindergarteners*. Slowly the title has been changed to that of teacher (for example, kindergarten teacher, nursery teacher). Paralleling this change has been a slow but steady increase in the expected level of preparation of early childhood practitioners, similar to the progression for elementary teachers. Kindergarteners were originally trained in a modified form of apprenticeship in training programs that were appended to private kindergartens. In addition to educating children, directors of kindergartens also trained young women to be kindergarteners. For example, Wheelock College in Boston and the National College of Education in the Chicago area, both four-year colleges committed to teacher preparation, began as private kindergartens with programs attached to prepare kindergarteners. By the turn of the century, a number of state normal schools had incorporated kindergarten training into their curricula and kindergarten teachers began to be prepared in these programs primarily to work in public-school kindergartens. Milwaukee State Normal School, now the University of Wisconsin-Milwaukee, and the Cook County Normal School are examples of this. Thus, the training of kindergarten teachers came to be closely related to that of elementary school teachers, as was their employment.

In the 1920s, a new form of early childhood education—nursery education—was introduced to the United States. Not only was the new institution called "nursery school" created, but the day nursery, which was designed to provide custodial care for young children, was reconstituted to become a more comprehensive child-care center, adding educational goals to its purpose of keeping children safe from harm. Rather than associating itself with kindergartens, the nursery school developed a separate life of its own in the United States, serving three- and four-year-olds while kindergartens served the fives.

The development of nursery education was spurred on by the evolution of the field of child study (later reconstituted as child development) as a multidisciplinary field of inquiry. As institutions of higher education established centers for the study of children, they often placed the centers outside of departments, schools, or colleges of education. At times this shift was influenced by the funding of these child-study centers. In the establishment of the Institute of Child Development at the University of Minnesota, for example, Laura Spelman Rockefeller funds were withheld until the proposed institute was withdrawn from the College of Education and established as a separate unit of the university. Thus, a rift developed in early childhood education between kindergartens serving five-year-old children almost exclusively, often in public elementary schools, and nursery schools serving younger children within the private-school sector.

Although early childhood education was defined as education for children from birth to age eight, it split into education for five- through eight-year-olds and education for under-fives. The under-five practitioners in nursery schools and child-care centers began to identify themselves as child development specialists rather than as early childhood teachers, and early childhood education came to be seen by them as "the practical application of the science of child development." Reflecting this, when a new credential was established under federal auspices for early childhood practitioners, it was called the Child Development Associate credential. There was considerable evidence in the discourse of the time that the group supporting the credential wanted to separate the early childhood field from that of education. (This trend now seems to have been reversed, with practitioners in child-care centers as well as in other early childhood programs wishing to be identified as teachers.)

During the long period described here, the field of elementary school teaching, and early childhood teaching as well, had been going through increased professionalization. The training of primary teachers increased from teacher training as a part of high school education to normal-school training beyond high school, and finally to training within college and university programs, with teachers in the public school required to have at least a bachelor's degree in a program specifically designed to prepare teachers.

Nursery school teachers have been and continue to be prepared in parallel programs. These programs may be found in home economics or psychology departments or in education departments. The standards for those preparing to teach nursery school and day care have not been that different from the standards for those teaching kindergarten or primary grades in these programs, nor have very different experiences been required, though the language of the programs has tended to accentuate what differences have existed. Recently, suggestions have been made to extend the preparation of all teachers, including early childhood teachers, beyond the bachelor's degree.

The field of early childhood education has grown rapidly; in the past two decades it has been splintered even further. The focus of the expansion during the late 1960s and 1970s has been on programs for educationally disadvantaged children and on child-care services. At the same time, though somewhat less obtrusively, public-school kindergarten programs have also expanded significantly. While kindergartens served less than half the population of five-year-olds two decades ago, kindergarten attendance is now almost universal (Spodek, 1986). Within day-care and Head Start programs, funded through client fees and limited federal funds, the concern has been with offering the most service to the most people for the least cost. This has resulted in minimal standards and low salaries for practitioners (Peters, Neisworth, & Yawkey, 1985).

Thus, there has developed a situation in which early childhood practitioners who are employed in public-school programs as well as in some private ones are expected to be prepared in bachelor's-degree or post-bachelor's-degree programs with proposed requirements being raised still further. At the same time, early childhood teachers employed in most schools in the private sector, or employed in federally funded programs such as Head Start, are being prepared in sub-bachelor's-degree programs such as one- or two-year community college programs, field-based CDA programs, and high school or vocational center programs. The trend seems to be that these requirements will remain the same and could lead to a greater split among early childhood practitioners.

PROFESSIONALISM REVISITED

In recent years early childhood educators have become concerned about the preparation and status of practitioners and about the disparities in the system. Calls for increased professionalization have been heard. While this would give recognition to the status of practitioners, it would also ultimately lead to the elevation of criteria for admission to practice in all early childhood programs. Parallel to this there has been an increased acceptance for identifying early childhood practitioners as teachers.

Suggestions for increased professionalization have not been accepted by all. Some have welcomed the trend, suggesting that professionalization is needed to increase salaries and improve working conditions of early childhood practitioners while increasing the field's status. Others have voiced concern that increased professionalization will cause a rift between practitioners and their clients, keep out worthy potential practitioners, hamper growth in the much-needed area of child care, and lead to diminished concern for child advocacy on the part of early childhood practitioners.

In reviewing the concerns related to professionalism in early childhood education, it is helpful to determine the sense in which the term *professional* is used. Often people use it to distinguish between someone who earns a living by engaging in an occupation and someone who engages in a similar occupation in a nonvocational way. Thus, a professional cook is one who works as a cook and earns an income by cooking. A homemaker who may spend a considerable part of each day in cooking or a person whose hobby is gourmet cooking would not be considered a professional cook. This does not mean that the professional cook is more knowledgeable about cooking or a more skillful cook than the others, for the opposite might actually be true. But the fact that one earns income from the activity leads to the use of the label *professional* for that one. In this sense a preschool teacher hired by a cooperating nursery school might be considered the professional in the school, even though some of the volunteer parents might be equally or more highly trained and even more skillful at teaching. While this is a legitimate use of the term *professional,* it is not the meaning generally intended in discussions about the professionalization of the field of early childhood education.

Another sense in which the term is sometimes used is to describe someone with a high degree of skill and competence. When one admires a fine piece of handicraft or a job well done, one might comment about it as a "real professional work." Such a comment does not mean that the work was necessarily done for pay, nor is the work thus described being compared with that of a doctor or a lawyer. Such a comment does not ascribe a high level of preparation or whether the person has had some accreditation to permit the work to be done. Rather, the term is used to reflect a high level of quality that is reflected in the accomplishment. This use of the term is sometimes seen in the field of early childhood education, but it is not the meaning generally given to it.

More often the term *profession* or *professional* is related to an idea that was originally embedded in the "learned professions," such as law, medicine, and the clergy. These vocations require a high degree of training in a liberal art or science and usually involve mental rather than physical work. Teaching, social work, and counseling are also often considered to be in the company of these more traditional professions. Because these latter fields usually require less preparation of their practitioners and often have lower levels of status attached to them, there are arguments as to whether, indeed, these are professions in the proper sense. Sometimes they are identified as *semi-professions,* that is, fields that have some but not all of the attributes of the learned professions. Each of these human services fields has made increased efforts toward professionalism, requiring higher levels of preparation, a more careful monitoring of the competence of beginning and continuing practitioners, and a higher degree of autonomy and self-regulation than currently exists in these fields. It is assumed that with increased professional standards will come increased status for the fields and increased income for practitioners.

While such a move is considered attractive by some, there are others who suggest that increased professionalization is inappropriate for these fields. Not only might it hurt the client-practitioner relationship, but the model of practice used may even be the wrong one. Some suggest that a model of *craftsmanship* would be more appropriate for many human service practitioners, including early childhood personnel.

The use of the craftsmanship model is not an attempt to demean or lower the status of the field, but rather to suggest that the "learned professions" do not provide an appropriate model for training or practice in the human services. These fields, it is suggested, represent forms of practice that are neither scientific nor systematic. The products of such practice are practical, but they are idiosyncratic rather than standardized. Craftsmanship, it has been argued, is an individual, expressive process. Such practice is best taught through modeling rather than through some rather academic process, even though there are distinctive conceptual elements to that practice (Eiskovitz & Beker, 1983).

Professionalism in education, it can be countered, relates not only to doing things well, but to doing things at the right time and for the right reason. Combs (1982) holds that professionals such as counselors, social workers, doctors, or teachers function in ways that need to be distinguished from the mechanical implementation of set routines. Decisions made by these practitioners concerning both their nonverbal and verbal behavior are based upon an analysis of the client's actions and the integration of such analysis within a broad understanding of human functioning. Such decisions are neither simple nor cut-and-dried. Decisions need to be made as to what is appropriate for a particular situation. The judgments made and the justifications for these judgments represent the characteristics of professionalism.

Given the history and diversity of the field, the arguments about professionalism versus craftsmanship in early childhood education may indeed be more intense here than elsewhere. Many practitioners have low status and low salaries. Many positions require low levels of preparation, and standards of practice may not actually exist. As recently as 1977, the Department of Labor's *Dictionary of Occupational Titles* gave day-care workers and nursery school attendants a low skill-level rating, on a par with kennel keepers (Hostetler & Klugman, 1982). Given the importance of these positions for our children, perhaps it is time to identify the specific expectations that must be developed for those who enter the field of early childhood education, to assure the public that such personnel have some reasonable level of required skills (Spodek, Saracho, & Davis, 1987).

The issue of the nature of preparation for early childhood practitioners (teachers) needs to be resolved. Should they, in the years ahead, become professionals, semiprofessionals, or craftsmen? Perhaps no one model can serve to define standards for performance for all early childhood education practitioners. It is clear that a variety of skill levels are needed in the field, with some practitioners functioning at the professional level but others not. The chapters that follow will help to clarify these concerns, providing a range of perspectives that inform the discourse related to professionalism in early childhood education.

REFERENCES

Combs, A. W. (1982). *A personal approach to teaching: Beliefs that make a difference.* Boston: Allyn and Bacon.

Eiskovitz, Z., & Beker, J. (1983). Beyond professionalism: The child and youth care worker as a craftsman. *Child Care Quarterly, 12*(2), 93–112.

Hostetler, L., & Klugman, E. (1982). Early childhood job titles: One step toward professional status. *Young Children, 37*(3), 13–22.

Peters, D. L., Neisworth, J. T., & Yawkey, T. (1985). *Early childhood education: From theory to practice.* Monterey, CA: Brooks/Cole.

Spodek, B. (1986). Introduction. In B. Spodek (Ed.), *Today's kindergarten: Exploring its knowledge bases, extending its curriculum.* New York: Teachers College Press.

Spodek, B., Saracho, O. N., & Davis, M. D. (1987). *Foundations of early childhood education.* Englewood Cliffs, NJ: Prentice-Hall.

2 • The Revolt Against Selfishness: Women and the Dilemmas of Professionalism in Early Childhood Education

BARBARA FINKELSTEIN
University of Maryland

Properly speaking, early childhood education is an undeveloped profession. On the one hand, a small number of high-status, well-paid experts—pediatricians, child psychiatrists and psychologists, university professors in education departments and in faculties of human development—legitimately claim a sophisticated body of theoretical knowledge about child development. On the other hand, the practitioners of early childhood education—nursery school and kindergarten teachers, day-care workers, and mothers—have been unable to assert "clinical authority," much less transform it into political, economic, or social legitimacy for themselves.

The guardians of children under five are among the lowest-paid, least-valued, lowest-status workers in the social structure. They exercise little control over licensing, access to, or regulation of the profession and enforce few meaningful standards. They exercise no important regulatory authority over the environments of children under five. More like missionaries than professionals, they command low pay for their work and, in recent decades, scant social recognition or respect. This chapter will explore this peculiar professional situation, paying close attention to the relationship between professionalism in early childhood education and the work of women in its development and definition.

The history and fate of professionalism in early childhood education are inextricably linked to the process of defining childhood education.

The author would like to thank Joyce Antler, Barbara Beatty, and Linda Kerber for good colleagueship, intelligent advice, and unobtrusive encouragement.

This process was undertaken in order to raise the status of children and child rearing, mothers and motherhood; to dignify social service; and to solidify the roles of women as moral and cultural authorities and as agents of social control and transformation. The women who became involved in the cultivation of early childhood education as a profession did not define economic or political status and authority as indispensable ingredients in professionalism. Indeed, several generations of women have engaged in the work of shaping the lives of young children in order to deepen the quality of their own spiritual lives; to engage in cultural, moral, and social reconstruction; and to enhance their capacities for intellectual and moral adventure. In the latter decades of the 20th century, they are doing it to earn a decent living as well.

Unlike the women who entered the teaching profession in the 19th and 20th centuries, the architects of early childhood education consistently identified material concern and political power as male provinces, inappropriate as professional concerns and inimical to the nurture of compassion in society. The development of this specialized definition of professionalism, and the particular role that women may have played in its evolution, is the focus of this chapter. Throughout, the role of women has been consistent. They have attempted to protect children by elevating motherhood, housekeeping, child rearing, and child nurture to a specialized moral status, and by equating professionalism with a capacity to discover the rules of child development and to provide good advice about how to promote it.

The concept of professionalism in early childhood education evolved gradually and in several identifiable stages. First was the period from around 1600 to 1850, when the concept of the modern family as a protective enclave for the young first emerged. This was also when special guardians for the very young and specialized institutions like the tutorial family, the public school, and the pediatric hospital were conceptualized (Aries, 1962; Cott, 1977; deMause, 1974; Finkelstein, 1979, 1984, 1985a, 1985b; Hiner & Hawes, 1986; Strickland, 1982).

Neither fully elaborated nor even consciously articulated, the concept of professionalism involved little more or less than the discovery of a specialized province. At that time, it did not involve the emergence of theoretical knowledge, political organization, controls over practice, or monopolies over authority. Indeed, the emergence of specialized knowers, specialized institutions, specific bodies of theory about child development, university departments, and moral and cultural authority did not develop until a later period, from about 1860 to 1920.

During the several decades from 1920 to the present, kindergartens (first appearing in the 1860s as private enterprises) have become a part of the public school, and day-care centers, nursery schools, and parent education programs have developed. During the 1960s, national programs like Head Start and Home Start gave new energy to the development of tutorial settings for children under five. More recently, the spread of proprietary day-care businesses has added another institutional dimension to the practice of early childhood education.

What follows is an exploration of the involvement of women in each stage of social discovery, institutional innovation, ideological invention, and social condition in which professionalism in early childhood education has developed.

REPUBLICAN MOTHERHOOD
AND THE WEDDING
OF DOMESTICITY AND POLITICS: 1750–1850

Among the more momentous developments for the fate of professionalism in early childhood education was the discovery of roles for women, and most particularly for mothers, in the nurture of good citizenship. It was during the century between 1750 and 1850 that womanhood was redefined, its image re-created and reimagined, its social function reviewed, its links to child rearing and socialization forged, and its authority over the moral and cultural development of the nation rationalized. The cultivation of a pathway to civic virtue was all the more impressive during a century when women held no property and exercised no political authority over their own lives or those of their children, and when child bearing, child raising, and unrelenting domestic, farm, and factory work constituted the range of vocational choices available to women.

One aspect of the redefinition of womanhood involved the discovery of new links between domesticity and politics. As historians Linda Kerber (1980) and Mary Beth Norton (1980) have suggested, women invented the concept of *republican motherhood* and created a new ideology and identity for women. Reflecting new ways of developing women's status, the ideal of republican motherhood linked the lives of mothers and children inextricably together in the cause of patriotism and nationalism. Mothers, through careful nurture and moral example, would prepare the rising generation of virtuous democrats capable of restraint and good judgment.

The preparation of women for this work became the ideological scaffolding on which evangelical reformers like Catharine Beecher and Lydia Maria Child were to build prescriptive literatures for mothers and new curricula for the preparation of women educators. At the center of their vision was a politicized household over which women would preside with scientific authority and social legitimacy.They would exercise power differently from men. Men would engage public issues, while women's influence would remain within the domestic and social circle. Catharine Beecher declared: "Whereas a man may act aggressively to achieve his goals, a woman must conquer by kindly, generous, peaceful and benevolent principles" (quoted in Sklar, 1973, p. 135). Aiming to create nothing less than a "national ethic of domestic virtue," Beecher helped to fashion two of the pillars on which early childhood education was to be built. First, she proposed that the character of women should exemplify domestic virtues; second, women should permeate the nation with their special character through their work as teachers and as parents. Thus, the traditional submissive role of women was transformed into a symbol of elevated moral sensibility (Sklar, 1973).

In the process, Beecher joined a growing number of Americans who glorified domesticity. They envisioned female influence as centered in the household rather than in the polling place or marketplace. They aimed to increase the importance and status of women within their separate sphere, rather than attempt to "dismantle the boundaries of the separate sphere so that women might mingle on equal terms with men throughout the realm of social, political and economic activity" (Conway, 1985, p. 63; see also Degler, 1980).

While women like Catharine Beecher, Lydia Maria Child, and Frances Willard symbolized and legitimated "domestic" or "enhanced" authority, or "social" feminism, they did not join the cause of abolitionism and voter rights being championed by those like Elizabeth Cady Stanton, Susan B. Anthony, and the Grimke sisters, whom historians have distinguished as "economic" or "equal rights" feminists (Agre & Finkelstein, 1974; Ryan, 1975). As Jill Conway (1985) has put it, woman's role in the shaping of the moral and cultural economy of society was elevated, authorized, and defined; her place in the voluntaristic, philanthropic sphere of the culture prescribed (Smith-Rosenberg, 1971).

This kind of moral evangelicism and female imperial pride led the champions of republican motherhood to serve God rather than men in earthly households; to devote themselves to the tasks of advising mothers, exploring child development, and filtering new child-rearing ideals through textbooks, mass-circulation magazines, and moral treatises; to create new spheres of authority for themselves and form new alliances with physicians, ministers, and an array of moral reformers seeking to manage social change in the first half-century of republican life (Cott, 1977; Finkelstein, 1984, 1985a).

Between 1750 and 1830, Americans redefined womanhood and, in the process, articulated a new norm and profession for women: protectors of childhood and children, and tutors of the young. As Mary Lyon, founder of Mt. Holyoke College put it, the nation required "a multitude of benevolent, self-denying female teachers," if it were to survive (quoted in Boylan, 1985).

Among the array of social reforms were those that distinguished infancy from childhood, projecting real differences between the needs of children under and over five years of age. As reformers viewed them, children from birth to the ages of five or six years old were under the control of animal impulses. Very young children required guidance, not repression, activity rather than confinement, and sensitive tutoring from a totally available, benevolent mentor (Deasy, 1979; Finkelstein, 1984, 1985a, 1985b).

Vulnerable in the extreme to corruption and overexcitement, or so reformers thought, young children required protection in the form of a purging of vulgar and debasing influences from their environment. The ideal protective household was a place apart, a retreat from the city, and from centers of ignorance and crime. Reformers articulated a norm of maternal perfection, a "maternal redeemer complex" (Mulligan, 1975). Mothers, by virtue of their inherent gentleness and moral superiority, were the proper agents of moral education. Moral nurture required the social isolation of mother and child and an intensification in their relationship. It also placed mothers in a position of strategic importance for cultivating the sensibilities in the child and for controlling the entire environment in which the young child would grow and develop.

This domestic environment was one where social, sexual, and mental precocity were proscribed and where children could develop "naturally," in a loving, carefully managed setting. Reformers called for a new form of moral culture for the young child, emphasizing the need for some physical and emotional space, rather than formal instruction (Finkelstein, 1985a, 1985b; Welter, 1976). Mothers ought not to teach their children to read but to drench them in sensuous experience, surrounding them in a world of natural and attractive objects. A romantic conception, the newly idealized family, involved mothers in close observation of children, in instructive conversation with them, and in organization of children's play (Kuhn, 1952; Plotz, 1979; Wishy, 1968).

An environment purged of worldly character, the domestic sphere of the reformers' imaginations placed a shield of morality around young children. The idealized domestic atmosphere rid the child of "premature mental exertion" and acted as a substitute environment for the schools, which they feared were making "intellectual machines" out of vulnerable children (Kaestle & Vinovskis, 1978; Strickland, 1982).

In an orgy of social and moral redefinition, reformers of the 1830s, 1840s, and 1850s did nothing less than project a new world for mothers and their young children under five. Between 1830 and 1860, the domain of early childhood education emerged. Children under five years of age were its subjects; mothers in the circle of home and neighborhood were its guardians; and moral reformers—physicians, middle-class women, ministers, and school reformers—were its specialized experts.

This "ideological template" was to acquire social definition and an institutional existence between 1860 and 1920, when two generations of women reformers gave birth to the kindergarten (Finkelstein, 1984).

THE INVENTION OF THE KINDERGARTEN: SPIRITUAL MOTHERHOOD AND KINDERGARTEN EXPERTISE: 1820–1920

Among the waves of immigrants who poured into the United States in the 1830s and 1840s were a group of social feminists from Germany who, like their counterparts in the United States, aimed "to exalt women to spiritual motherhood, as mothers to society and not just to their own households" (Allen, 1982, p. 319). For them the status of women was an important characteristic of the environments in which young children were to be nurtured. Freiderich Froebel was the spiritual and intellectual leader of kindergartners in Germany and the United States. He, too, tied the status of women and children inextricably together. "Women and children are the most oppressed and neglected of all. . . . They have not yet been fully recognized in their dignity as parts of human society. If progress and a greater degree of freedom depend largely upon the degree of universal culture, then it is women, to whom God and Nature have pointed out the first educational office in the family, on whom this progress depends" (quoted in Allen, 1982, p. 312).

The appeal of such sentiment was undeniable. Legions of women, led by Margarethe Schurz, Elizabeth Peabody, and Susan Blow, helped to create a new educational institution. In the half-century from 1850 to 1900, the inventors of the kindergarten worked with common-school reformers like Horace Mann and Henry Barnard, with philosopher/school administrators like William Torrey Harris and John Swett, and with social settlement organizers like Jane Addams. They cultivated links with the National Education Association and the United States Commissioner of Education, and they induced manufacturers like Milton Bradley to mass produce Froebelian pedagogical materials. Kindergarten pioneers managed to introduce the kindergarten to American parents and influential reformers and embedded romantic ideals deeply into the ideological foundations of education in the United States (Ross, 1976; Vandewalker, 1908; Weber, 1969, 1984).

Neither wholly domestic nor fully public, the kindergarten was a specialized educational institution, drawing children into a protected, quasi-public environment aiming to be moral and personal rather than cognitive and impersonal in its deliberate emphases (Finkelstein, 1985a, 1985b).

The kindergarten of the 1860s to 1890s was defined as an idealized environment, an extension of domestic nurture or the culture of the middle-class parlor, which was helping to produce morally autonomous, self-governed, self-motivated, self-disciplined, and self-controlled human beings (Cavallo, 1979; Weber, 1969, 1984). Viewing themselves as pedagogical midwives rather than drillmasters, engaging each child as a separate moral entity and preferring object lessons to drill, kindergartners institutionalized a new learning environment and in the process enlisted the frustrated energies of creative, energetic, committed, and high-born women in the work of educational reconstruction (Allen, 1982; Finkelstein, 1985a, b).

The rapid expansion of the kindergarten was the work of talented women who were committed to the infusion of the "mother spirit" into American life. Seeking to banish the strictures of Puritanical child rearing and prepared to steep themselves in the cause of child saving and moral reform in the cities, they carved out a dazzling array of educational channels through which to bring the kindergarten to the attention of Americans. Some, like Elizabeth Peabody, Susan Blow, and Kate Douglas Wiggin, wrote advice manuals for parents and teachers and contributed articles to a corpus of popular literature for women, created training schools, and themselves operated model kindergartens (Ross, 1976; Snyder, 1972; Vandewalker, 1908; Weber, 1969).

With rare exceptions, as in St. Louis and in several cities in California, 19th-century kindergartens were supported and sponsored by wealthy female philanthropists seeking to head off a "moral contagion," which they believed was overcoming children and women in cities. The kindergarten, like the social settlement movement, promised to bring moral culture into the slums, new child-rearing norms to immigrant parents, and moral and spiritual rescue to the ignorant poor. At the very least, they hoped to improve conditions in the cities, where poverty was visible and palpable, the children of immigrant families everywhere underfoot, and families in need of support and advice (Whitbread, 1972).

During the 1870s, 80s, and 90s, the organized kindergarten was, among other things, an educational adjunct to the organized charity movement, a special cause of groups like the Women's Christian Temperance Union and the General Federation of Women's Clubs. Kindergartens were especially useful to reformers like Jane Addams, who dotted her early writings with paeans of praise for their moral and social values (Lagemann, 1985; Ross, 1976; Vandewalker, 1908; Weber, 1969).

Kindergarten advocates knew the value of national visibility, professional organization, and public support. They transformed local kindergarten clubs into national organizations, creating the American Froebel Union in 1878 and the International Kindergarten Union in 1892. In 1885, the National Education Association created a kindergarten department, thus providing a new channel for the national diffusion of kindergarten ideals. By 1898, according to reports of the United States Commissioner of Education, 189 cities maintained kindergartens. Kindergartens and kindergarten training centers emerged in newly founded black colleges in the south (Cunningham & Osborn, 1979; Vandewalker, 1908; Weber, 1969).

In the first 70 years of its development, kindergarten leaders also began to cultivate specialized knowledge, to claim moral and cultural authority, to prepare experts, and to set up training schools to define professionals. They had bequeathed a foundation for the development and expansion of expert knowledge and of specialized institutions. They had cultivated a specific language to describe their work. They began to identify heroes and heroines and a tradition with which future practitioners might identify. Indeed, 19th-century kindergartners had begun the work of building a profession.

From 1900 to the end of World War I, these legacies were institutionalized as kindergartens became part of the landscape of public education, new experimental schools emerged, and colleges and universities throughout the nation established kindergarten departments (Cunningham & Osborn, 1979; Vandewalker, 1908; Weber, 1969, 1984).

There were significant modifications in kindergarten thought during this time. The near-total commitment to the Froebelian kindergarten was modified as psychologists, philosophers, and social reformers redefined its possibilities and purposes. In the first two decades of the 20th century, early childhood educators absorbed a multiplicity of ideologies, created a variety of institutional settings, and cooperated with a variety of experts captivated by the promise of child study. From around 1900 to 1916, an array of psychologists, philosophers, kindergartners, public officials, and social reformers worked together to dignify the cause of child study, establish a discipline of child development, create college and university departments, articulate norms of child rearing, create protective public policies for children, and dot the United States with experimental educational ventures.

Some, like John and Evelyn Dewey, were concerned with the effects of urbanization, immigration, and industrialization on the life chances of the poor and on the quality and possibility of democratic political life. They viewed kindergartens as important instruments of social transformation and nurture. The kindergarten of the Deweyan imagination, rather than a child's garden, was a miniature community where children entered, solved problems, shared environments, used materials from everyday life, and learned to control their behavior in accordance with the needs of the social group rather than their own consciences (Antler, 1983; Cavallo, 1976, 1979). Lazerson (1979) has suggested that advocates of the "progressive kindergarten" aimed to control the socialization of urban children. Whatever their motives may have been, the progressive kindergarten reflected a concern that went beyond the cultivation of moral individuality (Cavallo, 1979).

Beyond the work of social reconstruction that the Deweys projected for the kindergarten, psychologists like G. Stanley Hall at Clark University, and his disciple Arnold Gessell at Yale, organized child-study centers, developed questionnaires, and engaged cadres of interested mothers and kindergarten teachers in the careful recording of child behavior. Applying Darwinian principles of evolution to the study of childhood, first Hall and then Gessell cultivated a view of child growth as evolving in an orderly sequence. Aiming to cultivate a science of child development, Hall, labeling Froebelian idealists as "knights of the Holy Ghost," nonetheless affirmed the Froebelian belief in play as being more appropriate than book work for young children (Apple, 1985; Lazerson, 1979). Aiming to cultivate a science of child development, Hall invoked principles of health and heredity. He called for a curriculum based on an understanding of stages of development.

Like Hall and Gesell, Edward L. Thorndike aimed to elevate the scientific legitimacy of psychology while discovering laws of learning. Thorndike discounted stage theories, defining learning as habit formation and teaching as the construction of stimuli that would induce desirable habits of behavior. Early childhood educators like Patty Smith Hill at Teachers College were quick to initiate "conduct curricula," aiming to mold behavior in order to bring about "definite, observable, particular changes" (Weber, 1984).

A disposition to experiment, explore, and consider a multiplicity of approaches to scientific child study is evident in the work of the founders of private nursery schools. Joyce Antler (1987) has documented the tendency of nursery school founders to absorb all new ideas and to work with a variety of specialists in the years before World War I. When she founded the Bureau of Educational Experimentation in 1916 with Harriet Johnson, Lucy Sprague Mitchell worked with quantitative psychologists and measurement specialists; with cultural and political radicals like Caroline Pratt and Elizabeth Irwin; with social reconstructionists and pedagogical innovators like Evelyn Dewey; with those like Lawrence Frank, later to become executive director of the Laura Spelman Rockefeller Foundation and an advocate of applied psychoanalysis; and with Gertrude Harmon and Burford Johnson, who later became editors of rival journals: *Progressive Education* and *Childhood Education.*

The disposition to absorb different points of view was reflected in 1919 in the International Kindergarten Union's "Committee of Nineteen Report" (U.S. Bureau of Education, 1919). The Report contained three distinct sections articulating three different views of an appropriate kindergarten curriculum: one Froebelian, one progressive, and one middle-of-the-road model (Cavallo, 1976, 1978; Weber, 1969, 1984). Thus, for the first 20 years of the 20th century, kindergartners continued to absorb new modes of thinking about child development (Antler, 1987; Cravens, 1985; Weber, 1984).

The fruits of unanimity and cooperative endeavor were to become manifest in public policy in the early decades of the 20th century. The founding of the Children's Bureau in 1912 represented the assimilation of a child-protective presence by the federal government. Though not primarily a product of the work of university-based early childhood educators, the Children's Bureau received broad authority to investigate and report all matters concerning the welfare of children and child-life among all classes of people (Grotberg, 1977; see also Finkelstein, 1979, 1985b).

No matter what they did or where they did it—no matter whether they identified themselves as romantics or progressives, idealists or empiricists—the pioneers of early childhood education were indifferent if not opposed to the movement to establish women's rights. They assumed that women had a specialized role in American culture as agents of moral and cultural nurture, as child advocates, as social housekeepers, and, most especially, as custodians of the young. They created a norm of early childhood professionalism that projected women as spiritual nurturers who took joy from the work of social reconstruction, moral uplift, and childhood achievement and creativity. They popularized the ideas of educators like Hall and Thorndike, thus providing scientific authorization for women as natural guardians of the young (Biklen, 1978; Seller, 1981).

They were indifferent, if not outright hostile, to material comfort for women and ignored or opposed the women's suffrage movement that paralleled the development of their profession. There is no small irony in the fact that child advocacy became detached from the effort to raise the political and economic status of women, thus diminishing the material value of child work while elevating its moral and cultural status (Gonzalves, 1986).

The pioneers of early childhood education bequeathed an ambiguous professional legacy. On the one hand, they had developed a systematic body of theoretical knowledge, an effective political coalition, a group of committed professionals, a multiplicity of training institutes, and a new educational institution—the kindergarten. On the other hand, they had passed along an ideology celebrating separate spheres, distinct abilities, and spiritual rather than material rewards for women, and protection rather than rights for children.

PROFESSIONALISM AND THE SPECIALIZATION OF THE SPHERES, 1920–1980

A tripartite legacy—the tolerance of intellectual ambiguity, a delight in institutional diversity, and a commitment to the cultivation of separate spheres and abilities for men and women—was to persist as the field continued to develop from 1920 to 1980. The legacy was to become a professional straight-jacket when, as it happened, universities became indispensable agencies for the conferring of professional status. Beginning in the late 1890s, modern universities emerged as centers for the production of knowledge, the pursuit of scientific understanding, and the cultivation of technical experts. They continue in these roles today.

Increasingly seeking to develop "monopolies of credibility" and to exercise greater control over licensing and access, the universities have become linchpins of professionalization. University sponsorship has become indispensable in the transformation of fields of study into powerful professions, and of scholars and scientists into academic specialists trained in a discipline (Bledstein, 1976; Larson, 1979).

For early childhood educators, committed to no particular discipline and wedded to social reform, child protection, and creative pedagogy, the processes of professionalization undermined the very characteristics from which they had derived their sense of professionalism and dignity. What is more, the purpose of the research-oriented university was increasingly incompatible with the commitments of early childhood educators to spiritual and moral nurture, the cultivation of intuitive faculties, and the qualities of mind that had been identified as the special strength of women engaged in the practice of childhood education.

Within the universities, the world of early childhood study was to become a world apart. A variety of academics, themselves seeking status and definition for the social sciences, disassociated themselves from the work of child study, social reform, child protection, and education in schools, dismissing these efforts as the work of "reform crusades managed by giddy females bent on civic uplift" (Cravens, 1985, p. 437; also see Rosenberg, 1982). It is no wonder that early childhood educators in universities turned to measurement with a vengeance. The search for a science of childhood carried on in child-study institutes from 1900 to 1935 can be interpreted as a response to pressure from academic specialists who, in building status and power for their discipline, eschewed intellectual variation while sustaining belief in the intellectual incapacity of women.

Despite the hostility of specialized academics and the relative powerlessness of women faculty, the work of professionalization proceeded; but it could not and did not develop in the manner of other professions, exclusively through university channels. The trappings of professionalism in early childhood education—the development of theory, the cultivation of knowledge, the application to practice, the licensing of kindergarten teachers—were to develop independently of the universities, through the political agencies of an invisible army of women, directors of nursery schools, and political pressure groups comprised mainly of women (Antler, 1987; Cravens, 1985; Finkelstein, 1985a; Weiss, 1985).

The qualities of professionalism that emerged in the 1920s, 30s, and 40s and persisted for the next half-century reflected the social and ideological vision of philanthropic managers like Lawrence Frank, who presided over the Laura Spelman Rockefeller Foundation. Troubled by fractures developing between academic specialists and advocates of child study, Frank envisioned the creation of a cadre of professional experts who would wed research and child study, develop principles and practice of child guidance, and serve the nation as parent education specialists. Frank's vision resonated with a disposition to reconcile simultaneous commitments to research and public service. It represented a form of professionalism that enabled child study to survive in the universities, research to continue, theory to develop, and norms of child rearing and good pedagogy to be made available to aspiring kindergarten teachers. It also represented no challenge to traditional beliefs about women as social and moral housekeepers who had special abilities in this area but small need for economic or political status.

By 1937, when the Laura Spelman Rockefeller Foundation ceased funding child-study centers, a research infrastructure within the university had developed, in schools of education, child-study institutes, departments of human development, and other applied psychological fields (Cohen, 1980; Cravens, 1985; Schlossman, 1981). Although research proceeded without the stamp of legitimacy from specialized academics in departments of psychology, sociology, and other behavioral sciences, it provided a place where women could engage in university work, maintain their commitments to social housekeeping and cultural and moral uplift, and enjoy a life of the mind.

It is fair to say that the cultivation of professionalism in early childhood education was importantly shaped by women acting as midwives to the birth of new psychological theories and possibilities, applying and transforming them within the laboratory schools over which they presided. There are few reports of the work of the women researchers and theoreticians who measured and recorded children's behavior while adjusting and readjusting the classroom environment in accordance with psychological theories. There is little written about Anna Freud, who transformed and modified her father's insight, developing systematic and brilliant applications to childhood education (Cohen, 1979; Finkelstein, 1985c). Nor is the work of Margaret Mead or Ruth Benedict discussed in authoritative histories of the field.

We know that women were "popularizers" who turned their classrooms into channels for diffusing new child-rearing norms and for developing curricula based on child-study principles. It is reasonable to believe that they were theoreticians as well. In major universities, in selected women's colleges, and in normal schools, women introduced generations of aspiring kindergarten and first-grade teachers to the principles and conclusions of child study. In the 1920s, 30s, and 40s, professors like Florence Goodenough diffused the theories of Edward L. Thorndike and Arthur Jersild, engaging in "one long orgy of tabulation" (Cremin, 1961, p. 181) which changed in focus from the measurement of behavior and the cultivation of habits, to the measurement of mental capacities and the evolution of intelligence (Weber, 1984).

By the 1940s and 50s, the assumptions and commitments of psychoanalytic theorists and depth psychologists intruded into child-study centers and departments of education. Female professors worked with male colleagues like Kurt Lewin, James Hymes, and Daniel Prescott to develop, apply, and transmit principles of child development and norms of child rearing originating with Sigmund and Anna Freud, Erik Erikson, Margaret Mead, and Ruth Benedict. The emergence of a mental hygiene point of view was transformed into a call for the introduction of play as part of the pedagogical armamentarium of teachers (Cohen, 1979; Cremin, 1961; Weber, 1984).

In the 1960s and 70s, female professors of early childhood education continued the pattern of their predecessors. Applying, developing, and channeling theories of cognitive psychologists like Jean Piaget and Lawrence Kohlberg, they rejected concepts of maturation and fixed intelligence and projected the existence of modifiable cognitive and moral stages, which they began to apply to a reconstruction of early childhood curricula. Meanwhile, they championed the needs of children, transforming a rising tide of feminism into advocacy for laboratory schools and child development centers in and outside the universities. They delivered testimony in Congress and assured mothers that healthy and beneficial child care could be made available in centers presided over by well-trained teachers. What is perhaps most interesting about the response was the virtual silence about the low status and pay of nursery school teachers, directors of day care, and mothers.

From 1920 to 1980, several generations of academic women, working with some sympathetic men, were to develop and apply the findings of child development to early childhood education. The knowledge that they were to generate, however, was neither systematic nor coherent. It reflected a variety of emphases and ideologies and a commitment to multiple disciplines and interdisciplinary approaches to the study of children. They had articulated no clear principles of child development, nor were they able to muster sufficient cultural and intellectual authority to assure high-quality environments for young children. Further, they still sought no higher material rewards for the practitioners in their field.

Outside the universities, women took major responsibility for "the making and mending of the social fabric" (McIntosh, 1985, p. 12). They generated national support for maternal and infant care centers in the 1920s and championed child labor laws, mothers' aid bills, and public nursery schools in the 1930s and 40s. They carried on their work in specialized departments of government such as the children's and women's bureaus, and they transmitted what they believed to be scientific norms of child rearing as they advised thousands of women with whom they corresponded. They called on female professors in the universities to prepare manuals of advice about infant care for mothers and in 1948 created a clearinghouse for research relating to children. They supported mental hygiene clinics in the 1950s; were advocates for Head Start, Home Start, and child development centers in the 1960s and 70s (Ashby, 1985; Finkelstein, 1985b; Grotberg, 1977); and drafted short-lived standards for day care in the 1970s and 80s.

Like their university counterparts, however, they made no attempt to raise the economic and political status of early childhood education practitioners, thus extending the peculiar professional situation that had developed by the 1930s: child advocacy detached from any effort to raise the economic status and professional autonomy of practitioners (Finkelstein, 1985c; Grotberg, 1977; Hawes & Hiner, 1985; Weiss, 1985).

A similar disposition motivated the work of women educators who were working mainly outside universities and public schools—the mainstreams of American education—and who developed nursery education. Beginning in the 1920s, nursery school became increasingly popular, as women began to work in wartime industries in the 1940s, support households, and, from the 1960s to the present, to seek work and status in occupations outside the household.

Unconstrained by the research ethos beginning to dominate the universities, unimpressed with the results of quantification, and in any case deeply involved with legions of mothers who needed and wanted school settings for their three-, four-, and five-year-olds, experimental nursery school pioneers like Lucy Sprague Mitchell, Caroline Pratt, and Elizabeth Irwin waged an undeclared war on technicism, moral myopia, and social conservatism, which they believed had overwhelmed the purposes and pedagogies of education in bureaucratic settings like universities and public schools (Antler, 1987; Cremin, 1961).

Continuing to do research, they deserted the cause of measurement and quantification, substituting a mental hygiene point of view and elevating psychoanalytic theory; they created schools and prepared teachers in a manner that they believed would further the cause of social reconstruction and liberate the development of the child. Unlike their colleagues within universities, the pioneers of nursery school education extended 19th-century commitments to social reconstruction and provided a model setting for the nurture of cultural and political radicals (Antler, 1987; Cremin, 1961).

Their concept of professionalism, however, focused exclusively on the quality of the environments made available to children. They appear to have been unconcerned with the material rewards of teaching. Like their colleagues in colleges, universities, and public agencies, they identified professionalism with the status of children rather than women, and thus made few attempts to transform their knowledge into material rewards, high professional status, and autonomy for practitioners (Cravens, 1985; McIntosh, 1985).

CONCLUSIONS

Early childhood educators are the recipients of a problematic professional legacy mired in a historical tradition of child advocacy; economic unselfishness; political powerlessness; commitment to interdisciplinary research; and narrow concepts of moral, cultural, political, and economic possibility for women (Schlossman, 1976, 1978). The legacy has come to disassociate the status of university professors from that of early childhood practitioners. It dispossesses practitioners of economic status and professional autonomy, implicitly projecting them as fit recipients for advice and, in the case of teachers, of some professional preparation without the promise of economic reward, professional independence, or social status. The model of professionalism in early childhood education is one that promotes knowledge of child development as an indispensable professional ingredient but discourages efforts to raise the economic and occupational well-being of nursery school teachers, day-care workers, mothers, and the variety of guardians who oversee the development of the young.

Early childhood educators are, I believe, caught in a definitional and professional double bind. On the one hand, they identify professionalism with the scientific application of child development principles to formal educational settings for the very young—kindergartens, child-care centers, Head Start programs—thus linking practice to professional knowledge. On the other hand, they fail to identify professionalism with the acquisition of power and status, thus failing to transform clinical authority into humane and just environments for young children. Until they find a way to demand economic and political status for children and their caretakers and to view themselves as intellectuals as well as nurturers, they will share the low status of children and command insufficient authority to advance their claims.

REFERENCES

Agre, G. P., & Finkelstein, B. (1974). Feminism and school reform: The last fifteen years. *Teachers College Record, 90,* 307–316.

Allen, A. T. (1982). Spiritual motherhood: German feminists and the kindergarten movement, 1848–1911. *History of Education Quarterly, 22,* 319–339.

Antler, J. (1983). Progressive education and the scientific study of the child: The Bureau of Educational Experiments in New York, 1916–1931. *Teachers College Record, 82,* 559–591.

Antler, J. (1987). *Lucy Sprague Mitchell: The making of a modern woman.* New Haven, CT: Yale University Press.

Apple, M. W. (1985). Teaching and woman's work: A comparative historical and ideological analysis. *Teachers College Record, 86,* 455–473.

Aries, P. (1962). *Centuries of childhood.* New York: Knopf.

Ashby, L. (1985). Partial promises and semi-visible youths: The depression and World War II. In J. Hawes & N. R. Hiner (Eds.), *American childhood: A research guide and historical handbook* (pp. 487–531). Westport, CT: Greenwood Press.

Biklen, S. K. (1978). The progressive education movement and the question of women. *Teachers College Record, 80,* 317–335.

Bledstein, B. J. (1976). *The culture of professionalism: The middle class and the development of higher education in America.* New York: W. W. Norton.

Boylan, A. (1985). Growing up female in young America, 1800–1860. In J. Hawes & N. R. Hiner (Eds.), *American childhood: A research guide and historical handbook* (pp. 153–184). Westport, CT: Greenwood Press.

Cavallo, D. (1976). From perfection to habit: Moral training in the American kindergarten, 1860–1920. *History of Education Quarterly, 14,* 147–161.

Cavallo, D. (1978). Kindergarten pedagogy: A review essay. *History of Education Quarterly, 16,* 365–369.

Cavallo, D. (1979). The politics of latency: Kindergarten pedagogy, 1860–1930. In B. Finkelstein (Ed.), *Regulated children/liberated children: Education in psychohistorical perspective.* New York: Psychohistory Press.

Cohen, S. (1979). In the name of the prevention of neurosis: The search for a psychoanalytic pedagogy in Europe, 1905–1938. In B. Finkelstein (Ed.), *Regulated children/liberated children: Education in psychohistorical perspective.* New York: Psychohistory Press.

Cohen, S. (1980). The mental hygiene movement: The Commonwealth Fund and public education, 1921–1933. In G. Benjamin (Ed.), *Private philanthropy and public elementary and secondary education, 1921–1933.* New York: Rockefeller Archive Center.

Conway, J. R. (1985). *The female experience in 18th and 19th century America: A guide to the history of American women.* Princeton, NJ: Princeton University Press.

Cott, N. F. (1977). *The bonds of womanhood: Women's sphere in New England, 1780–1935.* New Haven, CT: Yale University Press.

Cravens, H. (1985). Child saving in the age of professionalism, 1915–1920. In J. Hawes & N. R. Hiner (Eds.), *American childhood: A research guide and historical handbook* (pp. 415–488). Westport, CT: Greenwood Press.

Cremin, L. A. (1961). *The transformation of the schools.* New York: Knopf.

Cunningham, C. E., & Osborn, D. K. (1979). A historical examination of blacks in early childhood education. *Young Children, 34,* 20–39.

Deasy, D. (1979). *Education under six.* New York: St. Martin's Press.

Degler, C. N. (1980). *At odds: Women and the family in America from the revolution to the present.* Oxford, England: Oxford University Press.

deMause, L. (1974). The evolution of childhood. In L. deMause (Ed.), *History of childhood* (pp. 153–187). New York: Psychohistory Press.

Finkelstein, B. (1974). The schooling of American childhood: The emergence of learning communities, 1820–1920. *A century of childhood* (pp. 67–94). Rochester, NY: Margaret Woodbury Strong Museum.

Finkelstein, B. (1979). *Regulated children/liberated children: Education in psychohistorical perspective.* New York: Psychohistory Press.

Finkelstein, B. (1984). Incorporating children into the history of education. *Journal of Educational Thought, 19,* 21–41.

Finkelstein, B. (1985a). Casting networks of good influence: The reconstruction of childhood in America, 1790–1870. In J. Hawes & N. R. Hiner (Eds.), *American childhood: A research guide and historical handbook* (pp. 487–531). Westport, CT: Greenwood Press.

Finkelstein, B. (1985b). Uncle Sam and the children. In N. R. Hiner & J. Hawes (Eds.), *Growing up in America: Children in historical perspective* (pp. 255–269). Urbana: University of Illinois Press.

Finkelstein, B. (1985c). Education and the discovery of latency in early nineteenth-century America. *Journal of Psychohistory, 13.*

Gonzalves, L. (1986). *Theories of mental ability and the control of women's lives, 1890–1930.* Unpublished manuscript.

Grotberg, E. H. (1977). *200 years of children.* Washington, DC: U.S. Department of Health, Education and Welfare, Office of Child Development.

Hawes, J., & N. Ray Hiner (Eds.) (1985). *American childhood: A research guide and historical handbook.* Westport, CT: Greenwood Press.

Kaestle, C. F., & Vinovskis, M. (1978). From apron strings to ABCs: Parents, children, and schooling in 19th century Massachusetts. In J. Demos & S. S. Boocock (Eds.), *Turning points: Historical and sociological essays on the family* (pp. 539–581). Chicago: University of Chicago Press.

Kerber, L. (1980). *Women of the republic: Intellect and ideology in revolutionary America.* Chapel Hill: University of North Carolina Press.

Kuhn, A. (1966). *The mother's role in childhood education.* New York: Teachers College Press.

Lagemann, E. (1979). *A generation of women: Studies in educational biography.* Cambridge, MA: Harvard University Press.

Larson, M. S. (1979). *The rise of professionalism: A sociological analysis.* Berkeley: University of California Press.

Lazerson, M. (1979). Urban reform and the schools: Kindergartens in Massachusetts, 1870–1915. *History of Education Quarterly, 17,* 115–137.

McIntosh, P. (1985). Moving towards a balanced curriculum. In M. Goldenberg (Ed.), *Integrating women into the curriculum: Proceedings of Women's Week, 1984.* Rockville, MD: Montgomery College.

Mulligan, J. S. (1975). *The madonna and child in American culture.* Unpublished doctoral dissertation, University of California, Los Angeles.

Norton, M. B. (1980). *Liberty's daughters: The revolutionary experience of American women, 1750–1980.* Boston: Little-Brown.

Plotz, J. (1979). The perpetual messiah: Romanticism, childhood, and the paradox of human development. In B. Finkelstein (Ed.), *Regulated children/liberated children: Education in psychohistorical perspective* (pp. 158–193). New York: Psychohistory Press.

Rosenberg, R. (1982). *Beyond separate spheres: Intellectual roots of modern feminism.* New Haven, CT: Yale University Press.

Ross, E. D. (1976). *The kindergarten crusade.* Athens: Ohio University Press.

Ryan, M. (1975). *Womanhood in America from colonial times to the present.* New York: Franklin Watts.

Schlossman, S. L. (1976). Before Home Start: Notes toward a history of parent education in America, 1892–1929. *Harvard Educational Review, 46,* 437.

Schlossman, S. L. (1978). The parent education game: The politics of child psychology in the 1870s. *Teachers College Record, 79,* 788–909.

Schlossman, S. L. (1981). Philanthropy and the gospel of child development. *History of Education Quarterly, 21,* 281–299.

Seller, M. (1981). G. Stanley Hall and Edward Thorndike on the education of women: Theory and policy in the progressive era. *The Forum, 11,* 365–374.

Sklar, K. K. (1973). *Catharine Beecher: A study in American domesticity.* New Haven, CT: Yale University Press.

Smith-Rosenberg, C. (1971). *Religion and the rise of the American city: The New York mission movement, 1812–1870.* Ithaca, NY: Cornell University Press.

Snyder, A. (1972). *Dauntless women in childhood education, 1856–1931.* Washington, DC: Association for Childhood Education International.

Strickland, C. (1982). Paths not taken: Seminal models of early childhood education in Jacksonian America. In B. Spodek (Ed.), *Handbook of research in early childhood education* (pp. 321–340). New York: Free Press.

U.S. Bureau of Education. (1919). The kindergarten curriculum. *Bulletin Number 16.* Washington, DC: Government Printing Office.

Vandewalker, N. C. (1908). *The kindergarten in America.* New York: Macmillan.

Weber, E. (1969). *The kindergarten: Its encounter with educational thought in America.* New York: Teachers College Press.

Weber, E. (1984). *Ideas influencing early childhood education: A theoretical analysis.* New York: Teachers College Press.

Weiss, N. P. (1985). Mother, the invention of necessity: Dr. Benjamin Spock's *Baby and Child Care.* In N. R. Hiner & J. Hawes (Eds.), *Growing up in America: Children in historical perspective* (pp. 283–304). Urbana: University of Illinois Press.

Welter, B. (1976). *Dimity convictions.* Athens, OH: Ohio University Press.

Whitbread, N. (1972). *The evolution of nursery and infant education in Britain, 1900–1970.* London: Routledge and Kegan Paul.

Wishy, B. (1968). *The child and the republic.* New York: Teachers College Press.

3 • The Challenge of Professionalism: Integrating Theory and Practice

BARBARA BIBER
Bank Street College of Education

EXPERIENCE IN THE TRADITIONAL SCHOOL

To get in tune with new fronts that schools are facing and creating at present, it may be well to look back quickly on the established focus and principles of past eras, which were grounded in governmental standards for public education. I can speak for myself, recalling the early grades in the public school in Brooklyn that I attended some 70 years ago. The school would not rank well by our present-day standards but, good or bad, I fell in love with learning.

I had the advantage of parents who honored learning, much of which they had been deprived of as immigrants from European communities. I remember teachers as kind though distant, who were conscientious in helping us acquire knowledge but who did not think the intellectual frontier was open to us. We were acquiring information, not asking questions or freely articulating or expressing experiences of wonder or puzzlement. Classroom arrangements were formal, with rows of individual desks, each with its chair, and the teacher and her desk in a central spot up front. There was a doorway connecting to a neighboring classroom or the hallway. The principal was privately ensconced in his office, at a distance.

Psychologically, under the surface, the message was: Be formally controlled; obey. Competing for superior rank was endemic in the system. Maybe my positive feelings about school were grounded in being placed

I am deeply grateful for Edna Shapiro's generous assistance in preparation of this chapter as one more instance of our collaborations over the years. Her ideas and insight have made major contributions to the development of the viewpoint as presented.

in the first row, first seat. But there were frightening moments. One teacher's way of reprimanding behavior was to take hold of a misbehaving child's head and bump it on the desk that was right behind. This, for me, has remained a symbolic horror image for life.

It is interesting to look back and see the roots of adult personality in the early years. In the back of our classroom there was a closed space for hanging up our outdoor clothing. One day I remember standing there in front of a few classmates, imitating the way our teacher gave us directions for what she wished us to do and how. From my recall the children were amused. But it was my bad luck that our teacher was standing in the doorway. I feel guilty now, thinking I may have hurt her feelings. Was this a premature identification with the teaching role which was to take a major place in my adult life? The punishment was reasonable. She changed my classroom position to the first seat in the *third* row! I was too ashamed to tell my family and relaxed only when this basically benign teacher reassigned me to my former first seat in the first row.

Children who did not "make it" on the competitive academic level in this kind of school found psychological avenues for self-compensation. Some internalized self-images of being the lesser person, maybe for a lifetime. For some there were other avenues outside the school: the fastest run on roller skates or the best pitch of the ball against the stoops of three-story houses. For others there was the sensitive librarian who found the book that was fun to read but not so hard as the one the teacher was handing out in school.

What was the place for nonacademic activities in such a school? The children's participation in music, dramatics, and the depictive arts was an expression of the qualities they knew were expected of them. Accurate reproduction, verbally or pictorially, was the standard of excellence in art.

This traditional school pattern has had a long history. When we conducted a comparative study in four different schools in the New York City area in the late 1950s (Minuchin, Biber, Shapiro, & Zimiles, 1969), one of them was a public school not much different from the one to which I had been initiated. (Although the desks and chairs were moveable, they were never moved.) The major goal there was to guide children toward the mastery of the symbol systems of words and numbers. Books were primary; the outer environment might just as well not have been there. Fundamental skills came first. "When they are young," I heard those teachers say, "they lack power to reason"; and, "no matter how intelligent a child may be, he wouldn't learn a thing unless he had discipline."

Quiet, orderliness, decorum, neatness, and social conformity were criteria for a good classroom. Level of excellence, measured by academic scores, was the major distinction for the child. Understandably, competition for high rank was a major motivation for many of the children, often stimulated by parental values in this predominantly middle-class neighborhood. (We should recognize how much competition and high ranking in school still dominate children's activities, even though other values have penetrated conceptions of learning and teaching and the maturing process.)

Some 30 years have passed since we conducted that study. Traditional schools still exist, but there have been radical changes in theory and practice, some reflecting basic social change. Male-female roles are not as fixed as they once were. Women are admitted to the police force and men teach four-year-olds. Women, while mothering young children, take positions in factories, corporations, and public services; men, to a certain extent, adapt to taking responsibility for children and home functions.

As is to be expected, this social change has stimulated public responsibilities. Publicly supported institutions and private and religious organizations have increased the number of facilities for the care of young children. In New York, for example, institutions providing care for young children in groups have come to be governed by a licensing system. Increasing variation in family composition and cultural backgrounds has brought new challenges.

Recognizing education as a social influence, is it time to ask how new thinking and changed practice may interact with the direction of social change. Before venturing to speculate on that complex question, we will look first at the changing perception of the educational process per se.

NEW DIRECTIONS FOR EDUCATION

The question of how children learn and develop has been explored in the past and has influenced the design of classrooms, which were presumed to encourage positive development. When we think of pioneers like Rousseau or Montessori, we realize how different their images and concepts are from the "traditional" school as just described.

I am most familiar with the thinking and educational procedures developed by Lucy Sprague Mitchell and her co-workers, especially Harriet Johnson, in the Bureau of Educational Experiments, the City and Country School, and, finally, the Bank Street College of Education.

Mitchell's concrete images of what experiences school should provide for very young children developed over several decades. She began her career in the social services and then moved into education, where she focused on how education, when forward-looking, might alter some established fundamental modes of social thought and enactment (see Antler, 1987). She had a preferred social image—generally more democratic and progressive, unlike the more concretely socialist image of her colleague in education, Caroline Pratt. There was faith, call it assumption, that there is a better chance for a better world if education offers the child in the growing-up years the experience of freedom as an individual and as a mind—one that can think and question beyond immediate experience. Helping the young child to get to know his or her world was a two-way process. The observing teacher got to know the child. Techniques were developed both to respond to the basic impulses, often as conflicts inherent in being young, as well as to acquaint young children with the wondrous reality of their world. How? By providing first-hand direct experience in the early years as basic to the learning process:

> a chance to put a doll in a bed, cover it, and sing to it;
>
> to put paint on paper to make circles or squares, or the beginning image of a body or a face;
>
> to arrange building blocks flat like a train or high like a house, with a doll inside;
>
> be the one who sings a song while the others join in;
>
> enjoy being held up by the teacher to get a good view of the newly falling snow;
>
> explore—go downstairs to see where the kitchen is from which the food comes;
>
> walk on the street to the market to see prunes and pears and watermelon—lots of them;
>
> ask a question, as it takes form, to the next child or to the teacher, or even try the student teacher;
>
> or, when a little older, be the one who hands out pads to the children who come to the school "store";
>
> and, with it all, enjoy being introduced by the teacher to counting— the number system, and to reading—the symbol system;
>
> to learn how to control or divert negative impulses that disturb and distress, and gradually become a somewhat socialized being.

The observing teacher in this environment has questions to ask: Did the children have different individual ways of responding to this environment? preferences? enjoyment? hesitation? Were these individual differences still observable as the children grew older and knowledge and skills moved into more advanced stages? How, in what ways, and to what extent can a program be adapted to individual differences?

RECOGNITION OF LEARNING AND PLAY
AS A PSYCHOLOGICAL PROCESS

Learning is a complex process. To put it briefly, there is a growth potential to be fulfilled for which we can plan a more positive environment for young children than has characterized group care in the earliest years.

What were the assumptions about developmental processes that were the foundation for the program designs for children's growth and development and that have influenced the special quality of the relations between teacher and child? In this regard, the work of Harriet Johnson and Lucy Sprague Mitchell is exemplary.

Harriet Johnson

I wish to describe and discuss the classroom culture created primarily by Harriet Johnson (1928/1972) many decades ago, focusing on the basic thinking that underpinned her model for children up to three years of age. I believe that her work will prove to be a valuable resource in the current expanded movement of care for very young children in a schooling environment. The nature of the observation and recording was different from many of the research studies of the era. The material gathered in Johnson's study included direct observations of the children's varied activities and responses. She observed the "whole child" in a few successive developmental stages, responding to people and the environment.

The overall perspective of the educators of her time was a self-designated responsibility to fulfill the *growth potential* of children at successive stages, with respect to both their sensitivity to and responsiveness to environmental reality. In the climate created there was opportunity to follow impulses and then to search beyond the immediate experiences of the moment. The children used the environment to explore, to question, to imitate, to try out what was new. The teachers responded to their exploratory adventures, for example, with a warm smile when one of them had the courage to climb to the top step of the classroom ladder and triumphantly slide down.

Looking into the records and study of Johnson's observations of young children's play in 1928, I find valuable insight into the growth process of the early years. The materials provided were varied but not always specifically symbolized, and they left room for children's projections of the images and meanings of their own experience. Their self-initiated use of blocks, crayons, dolls, and wagons became a way of projecting reality in symbolic form, such as a house built with blocks or an almost human figure with crayons on drawing paper. This free expressive experience registered psychologically; to the children play was a way of learning that always offered a chance to try another way if one way didn't work. It was a way of reliving all kinds of feelings, from those engendered by a doll nestled in layers of covers to those felt in pushing one small cat figure out of the enclosure that held other cat figures.

I am now glad to see that free play, in its early forms, is recognized for its importance as an exploratory, self-initiated mode of learning and also a way of building a fantasied world in which children can express good and bad feelings.

There is a question to ask about this "free" environment: What about *language and thinking*? Johnson (1928/1972) noted that talking was a natural ingredient in free play, especially when two children engaged in play experience as joint activity. It was also part of the ongoing questioning and explaining that was the natural interchange between teacher and children. This kind of free use of language both served and embellished the play activity for the children, adding a level of stimulation to the thinking processes. These teachers enjoyed thinking about thinking, both how to recognize its emerging expression and how to stimulate it as integral to the child's ongoing experience. How-and-why thinking was encouraged even in these early years. The young child has his own think-ing to do: "If those are his boots, they are not mine." The teacher asked, "Which is your favorite story? What do you like about it?" "Do you see how the snow on the window melts as soon as the sun comes out?"

Regardless of the apparent success of any such program, there are key questions to ask and answer. How much freedom should there be for expression of impulses in early years? How much control? These were not easily answered in Harriet Johnson's time, nor are they in ours. Miss Johnson theorized and put into practice a balanced program with its own psychological ethos. She believed in fostering spontaneity; in offering free choices of what to play and with whom to play and relate; in providing a communicating teacher who enjoys relating to a child as an individual; and in providing materials suitable to expression of young thinking and feeling. At the same time, she cautioned against creating a laissez-faire community so free that young children do not have some basic learning experience with which to control those impulses that, when freely expressed, work negatively on self and others. She understood that the teacher's choices, decisions, and style of exercising control create the special culture of each group. Of importance is the way the teacher, as an individual with his or her own lifetime experience in balancing freedom and control, translates the philosophy into practice.

The research approach of the program I have been describing had as distinct a design as its educational structure. The child was observed and recorded continuously in the ongoing setting of the classroom, in relation to multiple areas such as language, social interaction, reaction to stimulation or frustration, and so forth. Periodically, study of consecutive records made it possible to distinguish individual patterns and changes over time that bespoke the course and direction of the child's ongoing growth and development. This "whole child" approach to study of these young children's interactions with the "natural setting" of the classroom was quite a different technique from the more recent systematic studies focused on separate areas of response to stimulation, relying on successive administration of formal tests as measures of stages of development.

When shared with the teachers, this kind of recording stimulated the teachers to become thinking observers themselves, asking questions about the children which would be answered by more focused observation: Is Allen more readily responsive when I clearly call out his name? Does Jeanie remain consistently hesitant to try something new, even when I initiate the first steps?

As a summary of Harriet Johnson's contribution I would like to quote from my introductory essay to the 1972 republication of her book:

> In her interest in sequential ordering of observational material, in the importance of process over product of experience, in her conviction that the child should be creatively involved in learning, and exposure to new experience be kept relevant in meaning and form to the child's existing repertoire of skills and interests and in her ideas for a learning setting that should support the gradual transition from sensory-motor to representative functioning, she is placed clearly as a forerunner of developmental psychology. (p. xxv)

Present-day observing teachers can readily respond to her other insights related to the developmental process. For example, she observed that developed patterns of response are not sustained consistently, so that one may observe, for example, that the production of balanced colors placed on drawing paper may be followed with haphazard scribbling. Also, the rate of maturing is not necessarily consistent in all aspects of development; for example, maturing language usage is not necessarily paralleled with advancing motor abilities.

Lucy Sprague Mitchell

In Lucy Sprague Mitchell's image of what is desirable experience for somewhat older children (Mitchell, 1950), we find an extension of Harriet Johnson's principles and practices. They shared a common concern for planning curriculum design in relation to developmental stages while at the same time providing stimulation that increased the child's sensitivity to the surrounding world. This called for more opportunities for exploring and discovering how things work. To progressive educators such as Mitchell, this meant enriching the potential psychological space between question and answer with experiences that would stimulate wonder and create an explorer orientation in the child's psyche.

How does such a goal show itself when enacted in a curriculum? We see the child absorbed in watching the turtle, asking himself, "Why doesn't the turtle move around in the tank? What will he do if I shout to him? Should I sing to him? I'll try." Or, "Do the squirrels we have seen in the park hide in cold weather? Is it the noise we make that makes them climb up the trees? Would it be different if we were quiet? Who knows?" A varied program of what Mitchell (1950) called, "direct experience" at this stage, stimulating the children's emerging concrete thinking style toward discovering relationships, while also sharpening the observing eye, is seen as a positive direction for this stage.

Another move in a similar direction, stimulating the thinking processes toward discovering relationships, was the replacement of the commonly used recitation method by group discussion. A question raised in the circle of children sitting with each other is a beginning, another form of search, a thinking experience for the group. Within this social process there are times when an answer will be agreed upon; at other times, a plan will be made for how to search out an answer (such as to question about the squirrels in the park).

There was further progressive thinking in Mitchell's (1950) conception of appropriate experience for six- to seven-year-old children. The school, in her view, should carry responsibility for the whole child—body, mind, emotion. A good part of this responsibility she saw as invested in the way the play life of the child was to be understood and encouraged. Play was a learning tool that was suited to the idioms of early childhood, when the child is engaged in a cognitive search for relationships within the bounds of his or her personal experience. The child's reliving of experience takes varied forms in this symbolic medium of play. Sometimes it is a roundabout of personal relationships—love, hate, fear; sometimes an image of reality experience created according to the child's imaginative inner restructuring of outer experience.

The child's imagery is composed of the way things look, what happens, how people act, and unexpected things, good or bad, that often happen and the feelings that accompany all of this. Mitchell's perception illuminates the dynamic quality of the play process of these young children, which she calls "outgo after intake." This phrase conjoins the reality and fantasy aspects of the child's experience and ascribes to "play" a depth of psychological experience of which teachers are often unaware. In her words, "The era of educational exploration is far from over. Of course, it should never be over. When educators cease to be explorers, learners, they cease to be educators" (Mitchell, 1953).

Lucy Mitchell and Harriet Johnson were pioneering a new form of education for young children. Theory and practice were woven together. Today, theory and practice are separate provinces; seldom does the same individual operate in both. Often they don't even talk to each other. New lines of connection and communication must be built from both domains.

NEW FRONTIERS

Following the era when Johnson's and Mitchell's open-minded thinking was making a salient contribution to the conception and enactment of group education for very young children, there was a period that saw a broadened interest in designing appropriate models.

In progressive schools, moving with forward-looking thinking, awareness of the unconscious processes was of common interest though it was applied in different ways. For some of us, the position taken by Susan Isaacs (1930, 1933) on how teachers could use this deepened understanding provided some guidance on this complex problem. We believed that the school should supply an outlet for unconscious wishes and fantasies as one is opened up when there is provision for free imaginative play, and that there is an advantage when the teacher is aware of this process. She advocated the "opportunity for free unhindered imaginative play not only as a means to discover the world but also as a way to reach psychic equilibrium, in working through wishes, fears, and fantasies so as to integrate them into a living personality." She also distinguished the teacher's role from the analyst's role: "It is the teacher's role to attract mainly the forces of love, to be the good but regulating parent, to give opportunity to express aggression but in modified form, and not to attract to herself the negative explosive reactions of hatred and oppression" (Biber, 1984, p. 297).

An important influence on educational theory and practice also came from newly activated interest in education on the part of psychologists, especially those who were moving ahead to illuminate the changes associated with successive developmental periods and recognize the importance of the earliest years. Because psychological theory moves in more than one direction, as would be expected, there developed different projected designs for experimental educational programs, built on one or another preferred perspective. For some, new insight into the role of children's emotional processes, illuminated by teachers' awareness of psychodynamic factors, influenced teachers' response to children's problems. For others, interest in supporting cognitive processes influenced the kind of thinking problems designed for the child's learning experience in school. For some, both psychologists and educators, there was prime interest in curriculum that supported the ongoing interaction of emotional and intellectual processes, an awareness that influences the composition of experience provided for the children, and adds insight for the teacher in adapting his or her role. New images of what early schooling could or should be were taking shape in the development of these experimental programs, leaning to one or another psychological perspective.

In this same period there was a major movement focused on meeting the needs of the young children in families where mothers, because of stringent family support problems, were themselves working outside the home. In earlier years educators active in social movements such as the Works Progress Administration had proposed higher standards for the care of young children. During World War II many of us had worked closely with the New York City Health Department, formulating and disseminating standards for child care. It was an institution known for enlisting highly trained members and providing service with understanding of problems at the highest level. Similarly, in the Day Care Division, standards moved upward relating to, for example, the regulation that a group of three-year-olds was limited to a certain number of children and there was expectation of training for caretakers.

In 1965, the Head Start program was established as a nationally funded program to counteract the developmental disadvantages of growing up under conditions of poverty. Highly developmental in its emphasis, Head Start had comprehensive goals toward supporting and enriching children's physical and academic levels of competence, along with an equal awareness and interest in fostering social-emotional development and feelings of self-worth. While basic goals were held in common, Head Start programs varied in the ways in which goals were interpreted in establishing ongoing practice in individual centers.

Follow-up studies of children who moved from Head Start into public schools (Darlington, Royce, Snipper, Murray, & Lazar, 1980) have showed evidence of long-lasting positive effects of the Head Start experience, which has helped to maintain government support for the program. This generally positive view is somewhat dampened when one realizes that the amount of government support is adequate to care for only about 20% of eligible children.

INTEGRATING THEORY AND PRACTICE

It is time to move beyond the period of insight on the part of teachers to the period when (1) the question of teaching in early childhood enlisted the thinking and research programs of accomplished teacher educators and psychologists, and (2) enlistment of these professionals opened up new levels of thinking among teachers about program planning and teacher role in early education.

Among psychologists there were differing views, not only theoretically, but also with respect to their application to the educational system. In general the movement of psychological insight into educational experience is recognized as an advantage, but the process of conjoining psychological insight and educational procedure is not always clear. I have appreciated Bernard Spodek's view that "theories alone are not per se adequate foundation for curriculum building" (1970, pp. 48–59). He takes the position that they should be recognized as areas of knowledge to be used as resources in curriculum building, rather than as direct sources.

And also, some basic disagreement among professional groups should not lessen our awareness that all are sincerely headed toward making learning and experience in the early years a sound foundation for positive growing up and then taking a positive place as an adult in a complex world. This brings us to considering three different current theoretical perspectives in our own era on the basis of which different educational programs are designed and put into practice.

Behavioristic View

The behavioristic learning theory approach focuses on techniques that will lead to change in behavior. In a broad view the underlying goal reflects adherence to traditional concepts of education and standards for what is desirable, acceptable behavior in the classroom. This desirable, socially conforming behavior is part of the structure of relatively circumscribed academic standards. Basically, the psychological method is reinforcement of desirable behavior and inattention to the undesirable. What is right? What is wrong? becomes a dominant way of thinking about behavior by the children in response to the specific discriminatory responses they get from the authoritative adults.

The reinforcement of good behavior varies from praise from the teacher to more specific awards presumably attractive to the children— candy, access to favored toys, recess opportunities, or specific tokens of praise. The behavioristic technology focuses on "analysis of input and output in discrete units, observable and measurable and on a selection of 'target behaviors' that can be handled in such terms; it promotes an emphasis on product rather than process; on isolated responses or behaviors rather than the whole pattern within and across time periods; on forms of learning that are readily susceptible to quantitative measurement" (Biber, 1984, p. 282).

Cognitive-Developmental View

One of the most significant influences on early education when new directions were first opening up came from the cognitive-developmental approach conceptualized by Jean Piaget (1950). According to his theory, the child is basically an active organism, and learning is a developing process of maturing which reflects the nature of his environmental experience. For support and stimulation of early learning and thinking processes the child should have an environment that is sensitive to his tendency to explore, to try out, to take initiative, to pose problems to himself. What doesn't come out as expected merely presents new opportunities to try another way. And underlying the new action there is also the wondering question, whether formulated or not: Why didn't it work?

The question—why didn't it work—has a life of its own in this setting, related to the role of the teacher who, instead of instructing or offering smooth answers, stimulates further questioning while guiding the child to finding answers on his own. Thus, to a degree, the child becomes the agent of his own learning, a process that moves through four advancing major stages in cognitive development, divided in sequence and described by Piaget as qualitatively different one from the other.

Translation of Piaget's psychological theory into the teacher's practice does not follow a smooth path. What balance shall the teacher create between encouraging self-initiated activity and the course of leading to mastery of organized skills and elaborating conceptualization? It is not surprising that forward-looking educators, for example, Lavatelli and Kamii, who built programs based on Piagetian principles, did not always agree on the course of translation from theory to practice. The basic values for this orientation have been clearly stated: "to foster the child's sense of himself as an autonomous learner, a questioner, an explorer, a problem solver; his sense of the teacher as a guide, helper and source of information rather than authoritarian figure . . . his sense of school as a democratic social system in which exchange with peers is as highly valued as any other endeavor" (Biber, 1984, p. 286).

Looking back, it is not surprising that the Piaget volumes kept disappearing from the Bank Street College library shelves. Students and instructors were interested in tracing what this view shared with the earlier Johnson-Mitchell thinking, and where it extended into other directions.

The Developmental-Interaction Approach

This brings me to a related but different approach—the developmental-interaction approach, which has evolved over several decades. One can see how essential elements of what is preferred contemporary functioning are related to the progressive educational ideology of the John Dewey period. In moving toward a contemporary psychological position this approach now represents an integration of cognitive-developmental stage concepts and ego psychology formulations and insights—the developmental-interaction perspective (see Biber, 1977; Shapiro & Biber, 1972).

Our images of the growing-up child are multiple. We see him growing up in his awareness of people and things and in his ways of speaking and making things happen. In practice, this means that children are guided by the teacher as they engage in exploring their environment, within the school and beyond. This experience, which does not always pass by pleasurably, becomes prime material for stimulating cognitive processes—for thinking about what has been experienced. The teacher does not "teach." She or he relates to the direct experience that the children are having, stimulates differentiated observation, and presents questions drawing on concrete experience. Such questions are often in why, wherefore and wherefrom form that calls for further observation. In the varied areas of learning and cognitive functioning the teacher finds ways of stimulating thinking while drawing on ongoing experience. For example, in the course of story reading, she or he opens up questions about what may still come in the story; in preplanning how to clarify concepts—such as part and whole or same and different—she or he uses objects and events familiar to the children, asking, for example, how is a red ball the same as a blue ball?

In addition to using the experiential context as material for stimulating conceptual organization, this approach nurtures intuitive processes involving feeling and emotion. It recognizes the importance of engaging in reflection in addition to planning for action, and offers children opportunity to express their fantasies, free from pressure to duplicate reality. The importance of the opportunity and the setting for free play in early childhood is being increasingly recognized. Here, too, the contemporary interchange between psychologists and educators bears fruit.

This approach is distinguished from the other two in the quality of personal interrelations among those involved. There are social learning experiences for the children: organizing and joining play, responding in group discussions with the teacher, and settling disputes, all within established mores of social interchange. These processes are guided by the teacher, who uses understanding, explanation, and sympathy in finding ways of resolving whatever disturbance comes. Thus the children are learning what is involved in socializing experience, that is, what the psychological feel of give and take is like, what establishes "yours" or "mine," what can make doing things that are hard to do feel all right. Since there is no stern assignment of what is right or wrong, but instead an inquiry into why and how, the child is launched into the lifelong process of establishing his own value system.

The children initiate: They decide what to use as play material—blocks, human figures, animals, and so on; they decide what ideas of action or relationship to project, knowing that they have the freedom to move as close to or as far from reality projection as they are inclined. The play experience is the child's complex universe, and he or she uses it as such. It is a way of working through and clarifying concepts of what the real world is and how it works. For example, in the universe of block play a child can move a toy train across tracks (a row of blocks) into a more elaborate block structure (the station) and perhaps from there move to a different level and incorporate a toy figure that controls the coming and going of the train.

The play experience also opens up another universe for exploration: the child's ways of expressing feelings from the inner self. Examples include the enactment of pleasure (covering a doll with six blanket pieces); the fear of desertion (a single animal placed outside the block enclosure); the expression of conflict (a carefully built block structure of a house, knocked down).

The teacher supports the play experience, listens to the child's story of what it is all about when she or he feels like telling, and perhaps finds a new object to embellish the child's image. The teacher is also aware that the play experience is a self-initiated creative process in which the child can integrate his understanding of objective reality with personal meanings and feelings. As Biber (1984) states, "The child finds strength and pleasure in recreating order through his expanding thought processes, from sharing depth of feeling with teachers and children, and from recreating symbolically the meanings (real and fantasized) that are of the greatest moment to him" (p. 293).

The challenge to teachers lies in discovering how to use their deepened insight into the psychological underpinnings of child behavior and play in order to adapt and improve the learning and relating experiences children have in school. It seems likely that further observation of children's play could be a primary and useful way of understanding how cognition and affect, thinking and feeling interact during childhood and in later developmental periods.

TOWARD FURTHER THEORETICAL INTEGRATION

Of the three programs I have described, each has a distinct point of view about learning experience. Each perspective influences the course and the quality of the child's educational experience and the teacher's role in the school setting. In the first, the behavioristic approach, there are clear criteria of "good" and "bad" in behavioral terms, and specific techniques for reinforcing what is judged as "good." In the second, based on cognitive-developmental theory, we see programs of learning for the child that deepen and extend cognitive potentiality and the nature of relations to the teacher. The child finds himself in the kind of learning situation that encourages his own pursuit of answers to his questions and solutions to his problems. The third, the developmental-interaction approach, has moved forward in integrating understanding of cognitive processes with insight gained about the complexity of development by drawing on the contribution of psychoanalytic theory.

It is not surprising that the expanding interest of psychologists in educational philosophy and practice has taken several turns. There were differences related to both theoretical orientation and to images of how and which theory would represent progress if it could be applied.

Psychological thinking about early childhood education has at times been closely related to individual value systems. One example is an approach that was put into practice in several public schools under the leadership of Lawrence Kohlberg (1980). According to his philosophy, the endpoint of education should be the internalization of a mature code of justice for mankind. This goal influenced curriculum planning, which was centered around a cognitive-developmental viewpoint in which knowledge emerges through problem solving related to experience and a common process of thinking with others. Influencing reasoning processes was an important directive in organizing curriculum and defining teacher role.

Kohlberg formulated a series of sequential goals for the maturing process that were built on concepts of ethics and defense of rights in a democratic society. For example, for the preschool child at stage two, "right is serving one's own or others' needs and making fair deals in terms of concrete exchange"; for the mature adult (and not all adults achieve this concept of maturity), stage six "assumes guidance by universal ethical principles that all humanity should follow" (Biber, 1984, p. 302).

This theoretical system has not been universally accepted, since it appears inadequate as a guide for developing methods for the curriculum and an image of the teacher's role. Also, Kohlberg's emphasis on advancing cognitive-moral reasoning as the primary road toward the concept of justice has led to his dismissing psychodynamic theory and mental health concepts as irrelevant to the same goal.

I have referred to how Susan Isaacs integrated theory and practice in organizing programs that would both serve the realities of getting to know the outside world and create psychological opportunities for working through the positives and the negatives of the unconscious processes. Acquaintance with theory has an important place as a guide for practice, adaptable to continuous, thought-over observation but not as a literal directive for program design. In other words, "theory should not be insulated from application, nor should practice be allowed to escape responsibility for articulating theoretical foundations, since cross-fertilization is essential to sound progress in both spheres" (Biber, 1984, p. 304). This view was alive in other disciplines as well.

There was a period when looking at educational theory and practice from the perspective of developmental psychology became an active field. As is to be expected there were varied interpretations of the developmental process and implications for educational practice. Every general principle is enacted, of course, according to the way the teacher's personality, not only her understanding, fits with the role.

Briefly, it is interesting to note the different ways various psychologists undertook this challenge of relating educational practice and possible change to psychological theory. To Erik Erikson (1959), the quality of adults' relations to children in successive periods of development has lifelong influence. Denial of the expression of autonomous impulses at this early stage may become the foundation for feelings of shame and self-doubt. To Robert White (1963), the ego processes have intrinsic energies not related to instinctual drives. This view supports educational practice built on active, self-initiated, experiential learning. Other psychologists— Joseph Stone, Joseph Church (1979), Sibylle Escalona (1966), and Gordon Allport (1964)—made theoretical contributions to understanding the nature of interaction between areas of deep-lying motivation and emotion and the maturational theories of development, especially those concerned with cognition. From the title of a paper by Allport, "The Fruits of Eclecticism—Bitter or Sweet?" we can infer the complexity of trying to formulate a psychological theory that takes cognizance of the multiple and varied factors involved and the different interpretations of the processes.

The ever-present question is: How can we think about and sort out the different directions in which educational theory and practice have moved? I would like to review briefly some basic principles that have emerged. First, theory should not be insulated from application. Second, there is need for a comprehensive, overarching theory that includes the contributions of psychoanalytic theory, child-development studies, and naturalistic observational studies, as each has illuminated the complexity of personal development (Murphy, 1973). Third, taking into account that no theory may be presumed to be a universal truth, teachers should use theories only as guides for understanding, not as directions for practice. Moreover, theories should be applied only while taking into account the distinctness of individual development (Shapiro & Wallace, 1981). Fourth, researchers should become activists, taking part in solving real problems that bear relevance to actual classroom practice (Zigler, 1976).

These principles perhaps give a sense of both the general direction of thinking in this field and why that thinking sometimes takes different roads within a common value system. For Lois Murphy, integrating psychoanalytic theory and child-development studies is of primary interest; for Edward Zigler (May, 1976) there is need for more collaboration between child developmentalists and learning theorists.

Is there a common base for all of these activities? In answer I find Reese and Overton's (1970) concept of a "family of theories" clarifying, as they use the term *family* to speak about variation built on a common base. Looking again at the three programs in action which I have described, we can see the most obvious and basic difference lies between the behavioristic learning theory approach, which is based on a mechanistic-passive view of the organism, and the two other approaches, which are both based on an active view of the organism. Although the latter two approaches to educational practice are very different, they can be seen as part of the same "family."

There is added illumination in the way Franklin (1981) sees "the developmental-interaction position both as psychology of mind—incorporating psychodynamic and developmental concepts as a theoretical base—and as psychology of the person in its interest in the wholeness of thinking and feeling as well as the uniqueness of individual processes in reality functioning" (Biber, 1984, p. 306).

Perhaps it would be most useful to state the challenge in terms of the teacher who is needed to meet it. Stated simply, the teacher we are asking for is aware of the complexities of the interaction between intellectual development and affective experience in the developing years. Further, the ideal teacher is aware of the differences in the social codes and styles of interaction among young children from widely different cultural groups. Finally, we are looking for a teacher who can maintain healthy, cohesive group functioning which is so flexibly enacted that individual needs can be sensed, understood and met, with suitable adjustment.

REFERENCES

Allport, G. (1964). The fruits of eclecticism—bitter or sweet? *Psychologia, 7*, 1–14.

Antler, J. (1987). *Lucy Sprague Mitchell: The making of a modern woman*. New Haven, CT: Yale University Press.

Biber, B. (1972). Preface. In reissue of H. M. Johnson, *Children in the nursery school*. New York: Agathon.

Biber, B. (1977). A developmental-interaction approach: Bank Street College of Education. In M. C. Day & R. K. Parker (Eds.), *The preschool in action: Exploring early childhood programs* (2nd ed.) (pp. 423–460). Boston: Allyn & Bacon.

Biber, B. (1984). *Early education and psychological development*. New Haven, CT: Yale University Press.

Darlington, R. B., Royce, J. M., Snipper, A. S., Murray, H. W., & Lazar, I. (1980, April). Preschool programs and later school competence of children from low income families. *Science, 208*, 202–204.

Erikson, E. H. (1959). Identity and the life cycle: Selected papers. *Psychological Issues Monograph, 1*.

Escalona, S. K. (1968). *The roots of individuality*. Chicago: Aldine.

Franklin, M. B. (1981). Perspectives on theory: Another look at the developmental-interactionist point of view. In E. Shapiro & E. Weber (Eds.), *Cognitive and affective growth: Developmental interaction*. Hillsdale, NJ: Lawrence Erlbaum Associates.

Isaacs, S. (1948). *Intellectual growth in young children*. London: Routledge. (Original work published 1930)

Isaacs, S. (1972). *Social development in young children*. New York: Schocken Books. (Original work published 1933)

Johnson, H. M. (1972). *Children in the nursery school*. New York: Agathon. (Original work published 1928)

Kohlberg, L. (1980). High school democracy and educating for a just society. In Ralph Mosher (Ed.), *Moral Education: A first generation of research and development*. New York: Praeger.

Minuchin, P., Biber, B., Shapiro, E., & Zimiles, H. (1969). *The psychological impact of school experiences.* New York: Basic Books.

Mitchell, L. S. (1950). *Our children and our schools.* New York: Simon & Schuster.

Mitchell, L. S. (1953). *Two lives: The story of Wesley Clair Mitchell and myself.* New York: Simon & Schuster.

Murphy, L. B. (1973). Some mutual contributions of psychoanalysis and child development. In B. B. Rubenstein (Ed.), *Psychoanalysis and contemporary science* (Vol. 2). New York: Macmillan.

Piaget, J. (1950). *The psychology of intelligence.* London: Routledge and Kegan Paul.

Reese, H. W., & Overton, W. R. (1970). Models of development and theories of development. In L. R. Goulet & P. B. Bales (Eds.), *Life span developmental psychology: Research and theory.* New York: Academic Press.

Shapiro, E., & Biber, B. (1972). The education of young children: A developmental-interaction approach. *Teachers College Record, 74,* 55–79.

Shapiro, E., & Wallace, D. (1981). Developmental stage theory and the individual. In E. Shapiro & E. Weber (Eds.), *Cognitive and affective growth: Developmental interaction.* Hillsdale, NJ: Lawrence Erlbaum Associates.

Spodek, B. (1970). What are the sources of early childhood curriculum? *Young Children, 26,* 48–59.

Stone, L. J., & Church, J. (1957; 4th edition 1979). *Childhood and adolescence: A psychology of the growing person.* New York: Random House.

White, R. W. (1963). Ego and reality in psychoanalytic theory: A proposal regarding the independent ego energies. *Psychological Issues Monograph, 3.*

Zigler, E. F. (1976, May). Testimony to hearings of the National Commission on the Protection of Children Who Participate in Research. *Newsletter,* Division of Developmental Psychology, American Psychological Association.

4 • The Early Childhood Educator Revisited

MILLIE ALMY
University of California, Berkeley

Although it was published in 1975, my book, *The Early Childhood Educator at Work*, needs to be seen as an outcome of the expansion in the 1960s of early childhood education programs, together with the steadily growing need for day care for the children of employed mothers. Let me describe the role of the early childhood educator as I saw it then, together with the effect I thought it could have on improving programs for young children. After that, I want to raise some troublesome questions that need to be reconsidered as we try to move toward increased professionalization.

THE CONCEPT OF THE EARLY CHILDHOOD EDUCATOR

In the 1960s early childhood education became politically important as a palliative against poverty. A variety of programs for poor children developed. One kind, often referred to as "innovative," tended to be university based, research oriented, and carefully monitored by supervisory staff. Head teachers often had degrees in early childhood education, child development, or educational psychology. As time went on, aides and assistants were recruited from the community. Head Start, beginning in 1965, was much more deeply based in the community and involved parents more pervasively than had the earlier innovative programs. Head Start teachers, early on, often had little if any preparation in early childhood education or child development. At about this time the increasing number of employed women with young children, and the increasing needs of single-parent families, created a need for facilities to care for children outside the home. Proprietary preschools and child-care centers

I am most appreciative of the work done by Olivia N. Saracho in turning a speech into the written form of this chapter.

grew in number, often relying on teachers with minimal preparation. Approximately 900,000 young children attended licensed centers, while about 8 million additional children were cared for mainly in unlicensed homes of nonrelated providers (Almy, 1981).

One of the issues that the early childhood education field faced then related to how to prepare enough individuals to take care of and educate other people's young children in both traditional and nontraditional settings (Keyserling, 1979). These providers were needed to staff day-care centers and half-time preschools as well as family day-care homes for children of all ages (Almy, 1981).

The child-care center provided an extended day program, with children staying for as long as 12 hours each day; while family day-care homes provided programs for a few children, often no more than six, in the home of a provider. Although family day care traditionally served the largest number of children, it received little attention from teacher education institutions. Preschools usually operated on a half-day basis, sometimes for longer each day, but seldom were the hours for the children as extensive as those in a child-care center. Most centers served children ages three to five, the ages for which most preschool teachers were prepared. Training for those who would work with infants and toddlers was in short supply.

It soon became clear that the number of teachers who, on the one hand, had a deep understanding of children's development and learning and, on the other hand, had great skill in providing for such development and learning for young children in group settings was by no means sufficient for the programs in operation. The need to provide on-the-job training to improve the quality of programs was widely acknowledged and was eventually addressed in the establishment of the Child Development Associate Credential, beginning in 1973.

The National Day Care Study (Final Report, 1979), sponsored by the Office of Child Development (now the Administration for Children, Youth and Families), showed that "caregivers with education/training relevant to young children deliver better care with somewhat superior developmental effects for children" (p. 3). The study also found that because of the generally low level of pay, the employment of these workers did not raise the costs. Following preliminary reports from the study, efforts were made to amend the Federal Interagency Day Care Requirements (FIDCR) so that each caregiver would have a nationally recognized child development credential appropriate for the ages of the children cared for, or would participate regularly in training related to child care. Unfortunately, these efforts did not succeed. (See Department of Health, Education and Welfare, 1978, for the FIDCR and their legislative history.)

As I looked at programs in the late 1960s and early 70s, it seemed that a major problem lay in the fact that too few of the staff in most programs had access to individuals who could help them to improve. Those who had sufficient understanding of child development and sufficient skill in working with children often lacked the ability to teach others to deal with children more effectively. It was impractical to hope that every class of 15 to 20 preschoolers could be staffed with teachers who held master's, or even bachelor's, degrees in early childhood education. Suppose, instead, we could insure that every class and its staff had weekly access to an individual who was a graduate in early childhood education and child development and who had special skills in working with adults as well as with children. Such a person could get to know the children in five classes well through both participation and observation, could demonstrate teaching strategies, and, through comments and questions, would facilitate and encourage staff members to be more reflective about their teaching and their relationships with children and parents. At that time there were educational directors in privileged schools with about 100 children who were able to function in this way.

I did not limit my description of the role of the early childhood educator to that of being an educational director, but suggested that persons with the requisite knowledge and skills could also function as administrators, instructors and professors, and consultants in health and welfare services and in various commercial or industrial services for young children and their parents. I would like to focus this discussion, however, on the educational director as the prototype for the early childhood educator, since I think it is central to the issue of professionalism.

I described the early childhood educator as a "double specialist," a term first used by Sylvia Farnham-Diggory in 1972. This double specialty involves both teaching young children and assessing their development; both working with children and working with adults; both thinking concretely (as children do) and thinking formally (as researchers do), in practice and in theory.

The early childhood educator role requires professional attitudes and behaviors, although early childhood education does not meet the standards for a profession. With its shaky knowledge base, its ambiguous clientele, and its lack of a code of ethics, early childhood education qualifies only as an occupation or, at best, a semiprofession.

The possibility of organizing early childhood education and development programs so that every 100 or so children would have access to a person of professional caliber at least weekly did not seem too remote in the late 1960s and early 1970s, when federal support for such programs seemed imminent. Revisiting the possibility in the cold economic austerity of the 1980s makes me wonder at the naïveté of never assessing the costs of such an organization. On the other hand, it seems clear that, if a large cadre of early childhood educators had been available to help programs struggling to meet the increasing demands for child care during the last decade, we might now have fewer horror stories like those that currently beset us. Much as was done in the study, *Changed Lives* (Berrueta-Clement, Schweinhart, Barnett, Epstein, & Weikart, 1984), we should attempt to project the costs and benefits of the systematic introduction of professionally qualified early childhood educators into child-care and development systems.

CONTEMPORARY CONCERNS INFLUENCING THE CONCEPT

Presently, reduced budgets and widespread criticism threaten the training of teachers. Retrenchment is found in every teacher education setting. Teacher trainers, like classroom teachers, are burning out and running scared. In coping effectively with these circumstances, teachers and teacher trainers need to become advocates. They need to learn to work in collaboration with colleagues throughout the field and in related professions as well as with parents and citizens concerned with the deleterious effects of low-quality child care. They also need to become better informed about current child-care issues (Almy, 1985).

Aside from the issue of cost, a number of other difficult issues need to be considered about the professional role of the early childhood educator. Three of these are: (1) the effect of creating a formal hierarchy of practitioners within the field of early childhood education, (2) the provisions for access to the role, and (3) the knowledge base for the role.

The Effect of Creating
a Hierarchy of Practitioners

This issue has troubled me from the time I first proposed the role. In the present system, it may be explicitly acknowledged that child-care center directors have authority over teachers, and that teachers have authority over aides and assistants. In practice, however, this hierarchy often remains only implicit, as staff follow the early childhood education tradition of being a team, working together for the good of the children. In this respect, early childhood education, requiring the presence of at least two adults, differs from other levels of teaching where the teacher usually works alone. The authority of the early childhood educator rests in his or her knowledge and skills. The person functioning in that role must know how to work with other adults so that they feel valued as participants in mutual collaboration. Nevertheless, the early childhood educator role represents a career option that carries with it more preparation, more knowledge, and more responsibility than that of the classroom teacher and should, accordingly, carry greater financial remuneration. How might this affect the ways teachers, assistants, and aides view the role and the ways they perceive their own roles? Is it reasonable to assume that teachers, assistants, and aides may see their time in the classroom as part of a series of different career options? For example, one group may elect to remain in the classroom throughout their careers, another group may opt for experience in the classroom as preliminary to a different but related career, and a third group may opt for a career that culminates in the role of early childhood educator.

Provisions for Access to the Role

In my description (Almy, 1975) I suggested that potential candidates for the role of the early childhood educator would be found among those already working in preschools and child-care centers. I did not envision individuals planning from their undergraduate days to become an early childhood educator by opting for a graduate degree that would qualify them. I had hoped that the nature of their work in classrooms would mark them as individuals with the personality and intellectual concerns that the early childhood educator role demands. I was, and am, particularly concerned that members of minority groups and men—those whose classroom work reveals the essential qualities—have the opportunity to advance into the role. One question, particularly appropriate at a time when fellowships for graduate study are not plentiful, is whether advanced study can be effectively carried on while one is already on the job as a teacher or center director. That is the way many if not most people in early childhood education have moved ahead in the past. I am convinced, however, that some provision needs to be made for a period of time to allow for "distancing" oneself from the day-to-day realities and for reflection.

This relates to the issue of cost-benefit relationships. Perhaps we could follow up some of the teachers who participated in the early childhood education fellowship programs that were available during the late 1960s, to determine to what extent they, with their increased knowledge and skill, were able to influence programs for children. We must question, however, whether the knowledge provided teachers in those programs was of a kind to be most useful in the betterment of programs for children. Of this I am uncertain.

While we need to provide more opportunities for high-level preparation of early childhood educators, increased opportunities for training early childhood practitioners are essential at all levels. Such training can be done by early childhood educators who recognize that simply lecturing to practitioners about concepts is not enough. Adults, like children, learn by doing. Individuals, at all levels, can be helped to acquire a strong sense of their own potential. They can do this through reading books and listening to lectures and observing good teachers in practice. But hearing the ideas and observing good models is not enough. They need to practice and evaluate their own versions of what they learn. They can evolve new and better forms of practice out of their own experience as well as the knowledge gained from others. When early childhood practitioners are encouraged to go beyond classroom practice, they can learn to be advocates for children and their families as well as for themselves as teachers (Almy, 1985).

The Knowledge Base for the Role

My description of the early childhood educator (Almy, 1975) declared that the knowledge base for that role needed to be "interdisciplinary," drawing not only from psychology but also from pediatrics, nutrition, sociology, and anthropology. Since then I have learned from graduate students how difficult it is to acquire interdisciplinary knowledge and at the same time how valuable it is, both practically and theoretically. I also failed to emphasize adequately the value of knowledge of economics and politics. For too long, early childhood education held itself above the mundane issue of the cost of quality and how to influence others to think and act about the relationship of cost to quality. One of the advances of the last decade has been the increasing sophistication of teachers and others in early childhood education about matters that are essentially economic and political.

In another aspect of the knowledge base we have made relatively less progress: the idea that the major source of theory to guide early childhood practice comes from research in child development and learning. While child development can be a resource in developing early childhood curricula, it cannot be conceived of as the sole source (Biber, 1984; Spodek, 1970). The importance of this source of knowledge cannot be denied, but its limitations need recognition. Relatively little research is based on children and teachers as they participate in classroom activities. Instead, the researchers take children out of their classrooms to play games or to answer questions, or they draw on parents' or teachers' recollections of children's behavior. Rarely do the researchers observe what goes on in classrooms or playgrounds, to see what teachers and children do and say and how they respond to one another. Still more rarely are the concerns of teachers reflected in the questions to which researchers seek answers. We need much more collaboration between teachers and researchers, much more sharing of the way that classrooms look and feel to teachers, before we shall capture the essence of what the best teachers know and do almost intuitively.

There are those who believe that theoretical knowledge from child development should be the foundation for an early childhood curriculum. There are others who believe that the transition from theory to practice should begin with a value statement of what children "ought to be and become" (Biber, 1984, p. 303). The implicit theories that teachers use to derive their classroom decisions and actions contain elements of both scientific theory and value orientations (Spodek, this volume). Teachers have intuitively felt the inadequacy of child development theory as the basis for their practice and have sought to go beyond it themselves.

CONCLUSION

The early childhood educator, as I conceptualized it, still has promise. A cadre of early childhood educators, with qualifications of true professionals, has much to offer the field. But certain aspects of the role need more attention and rethinking. As we look toward the 21st century, early childhood teacher educators need to make a fresh start, considering the realities and complexities facing parents and their infants, toddlers, and preschoolers, and seeking coalitions with parents and with other professionals involved with families, examining the multitude of resources that could be brought to bear on the care and education of young children. New patterns can then evolve and the early childhood educator role can be modified to fit the new era of the information society.

REFERENCES

Almy, M. (1975). *The early childhood educator at work*. New York: McGraw-Hill.

Almy, M. (1981). Education and training for day care: Implications for child care education. *Child Care Quarterly, 10*(3), 226–241.

Almy, M. (1985). New challenges for teacher education: Facing political and economic realities. *Young Children, 40*(6), 10–11.

Berrueta-Clement, J. R., Schweinhart, L. J., Barnett, W. S., Epstein, A. S., & Weikart, D. P. (1984). *Changed Lives: The Effects of the Perry Preschool Program on Youths Through Age 19* (Monograph No. 8). Ypsilanti, MI: High/Scope Educational Research Foundation.

Biber, B. (1984). *Early education and psychological development.* New Haven, CT: Yale University Press.

Department of Health, Education and Welfare. Office of Assistant Secretary of Planning and Evaluation. (1978). *The appropriateness of the federal interagency day care requirements: Report of findings and recommendations.* (No. 017-000-00211-2). Washington, DC: U.S. Government Printing Office.

Farnham-Diggory, S. (1972). *Cognitive processes in education.* New York: Harper & Row.

Keyserling, M. D. (1979, March 2). Overview—Day care standards: Past, present and future. Paper presented at a seminar, Day Care Standards: What's Ahead. Conference convened by *Day Care* and *Child Development Reports.* Washington, DC. ERIC Document Reproduction Service No. ED 172 937.

Spodek, B. (1970). What are the sources of early childhood curriculum? *Young Children, 26*(1), 48–59.

Spodek, B. (1988). Implicit theories of early childhood teachers: Foundations for professional behavior. In B. Spodek, O. N. Saracho, & D. L. Peters (Eds.), *Professionalism and the Early Childhood Practitioner.* New York: Teachers College Press.

Part II

DEFINING
PROFESSIONALISM

5 • Professionalism in Early Childhood Education

BERNARD SPODEK
University of Illinois

OLIVIA N. SARACHO
University of Maryland

The last few years have seen an increased concern for the quality of early childhood education programs and the quality of practice within these programs. Teaching young children takes more than a love of children; it also requires knowledge and skill, which are usually gained in preservice teacher education programs. By improving the preparation of early childhood teachers we might be able to raise the level of professionalism in the field and improve the practice of teaching in early childhood education.

THE CHARACTERISTICS OF A PROFESSION

Professionals in any field possess a high level of knowledge and skill developed over a rather extensive period of preparation. The field's body of knowledge is drawn from research, theory, and practice. The knowledge and skill gained are used to perform a service for others.

Originally, the term *profession* was applied to the "learned professions" of law, medicine, and the ministry. Over time the term has been applied more broadly. Persons who engage in many activities as a vocation may be termed *professionals*. Auto mechanics or ball players may be considered professional, in contrast with hobbyists or amateurs, because they engage in their craft for pay. Greenwood (1962), an expert on professional occupations and organizations, maintains that a criterion for professionalism should be that the group establishes and enforces standards for professional practice and monitors its interactions with the public.

Some experts in the field of teacher education (e.g., Howsam, Corrigan, Denemark, and Nash, 1976) describe teaching as a semiprofession rather than as a profession. They place teaching within a range of occupational categories that include professional, semiprofessional, paraprofessional, skilled, and unskilled trade categories. They have developed the following list of characteristics of a profession, drawn from several authoritative sources (see Howsam, R. B., Corrigan, D. C., Denemark, G. W., & Nash, R. J. [1976]. *Education as a profession*. Washington, DC: American Association of Colleges of Teacher Education):

1. Occupationally related social institutions established and maintained to provide essential services
2. Concerned with an area of need or function
3. Possesses a body of knowledge and skills needed for practice that is not normally possessed by others
4. Members involved in decisions
5. Based on an undergirding theory
6. Organized into a professional association which has autonomy regarding the work of the profession
7. Agreed upon standards for admission and continuing practice
8. Protracted period of preparation in university study
9. High level of public trust in the profession and its practitioners
10. Practitioners have a strong service motivation and commitment to competence
11. Authority to practice derives from the client; accountability to the profession
12. Freedom from on-the-job supervision; accountable through the profession.

Howsam et al. (1976) suggest that, as semiprofessionals, teachers differ in significant ways from true professionals. They have lower occupational status, a shorter training period, and a lower level of societal acceptance. In addition, there is less emphasis on a theoretical and conceptual basis for practice, and the field contains a less specialized and less highly developed body of knowledge and skills. Teachers have less autonomy in professional decision making. They are more subject to administrative control, are managed by persons who themselves are semiprofessionals, and tend to identify more with their employing institutions than with the profession. Finally, Howsam and colleagues suggest that, as semiprofessionals, teachers are predominantly women, lack privileged communication with clients, and have little involvement in matters of life and death.

Ade (1982) also suggests that teachers in the field of early childhood education do not reflect the characteristics of a profession. They have lower status than do other teachers, although he believes that the field has the potential to develop higher levels of professionalism. Current developments suggest that the field is now beginning to establish professional standards for educators (Bowman, 1982).

One might question, however, whether all early childhood teachers can or should meet the criteria for being professionals or even semiprofessionals. Teachers in some nursery and day-care programs are often not expected to have the same level of preparation as elementary and secondary school teachers, the semiprofessionals that Howsam and his colleagues (1976) have identified. These teachers may also be paid significantly lower salaries than elementary and secondary teachers. In addition, adults other than teachers are responsible for the education of young children in the classroom. These adults have different responsibilities and perform different roles. Spodek (1972) refers to such individuals, including teacher's aides and teacher's assistants, as serving "auxiliary roles." In distinguishing these roles from one another, Spodek differentiates between the level of preparation required for each and the level of responsibility assigned to each.

The National Association for the Education of Young Children (NAEYC, 1984) has recognized varied levels of preparation and responsibility among practitioners. The association has identified four levels of early childhood education practice, describing the levels of knowledge and skill expected for each level and suggesting ways to achieve that knowledge and skill:

> *Level 1: Early Childhood Teacher Assistants* are entry-level personnel who implement program activities under direct supervision of the professional staff. This level would have a high school diploma or equivalent. Once employed, the individual should be expected to participate in professional development programs.
>
> *Level 2: Early Childhood Associate Teachers* independently implement program activities and may be responsible for the care and education of a group of children. They must be able to demonstrate competency in six basic areas as defined by the national Child Development Associate (CDA) Credentialing Program.
>
> *Level 3: Early Childhood Teachers* provide care and education for groups of children. They must demonstrate all Level 1 and Level 2 competencies and possess greater theoretical knowledge and practical skills. A bachelor's degree in early childhood education or child development would be required.
>
> *Level 4: Early Childhood Specialists* supervise and train staff, design curriculum, and/or administer programs. They are expected to

have at least a bachelor's degree in early childhood education or child development and three years of full-time teaching experience with young children and/or an advanced degree.

Levels 3 and 4 of this hierarchy might identify practitioners with professional status. While these levels have been disseminated by NAEYC, they have not been adopted as a set of standards for the field. Given the nature of the field of early childhood education in the United States, it is not clear whether any group has the power to insure that such standards would be widely accepted and that practitioners will be properly prepared for each of these levels.

Certification

Certification serves to identify those persons who possess the minimum competencies needed for successful teaching. A teaching certificate attests that professionals have a "safe level" of beginning skills with which to initiate a teaching career (Howsam et al., 1976). Qualifications for certification guarantee that teachers possess some basic level of professional knowledge and competence.

In our country, individual states establish standards to certify competent teachers. Different teaching certificates are usually offered for different levels of education or for different teaching specialties. In some states, the initial teaching certificate is a provisional one, with teachers required to demonstrate advanced study or successful practice before a permanent certificate is issued. While standards and qualifications for certificates vary from state to state, a general agreement exists on the following:

1. Authority for teacher certification rests in the state departments of education.
2. Certificates are issued to teachers based on specialization in particular subject fields or grade levels.
3. Certificates usually must be renewed periodically.
4. At least a baccalaureate degree is required for a teaching certificate.
5. Specific courses in education and in a subject matter or teaching field must be taken as part of the preparation of teachers. [adapted from Hughes & Schultz, 1976]

Colleges and universities have been given the primary responsibility for preparing teachers. They are not totally autonomous, however, since they must adhere to standards established by state education agencies and by professional groups.

Teacher preparation degree work normally includes (1) courses in general education, (2) general courses in the field of education, and (3) specialized courses related to the individual's teaching field. Individuals must pass prescribed courses and perform well as student teachers under supervision, providing evidence that they have acquired at least a minimum level of teaching competence.

Several problems are evident in current approaches to teacher preparation and certification. Teacher education programs vary in how they constitute their programs, offering different-valued program outcomes. Such differences represent the lack of an agreement about what teachers need to know. Problems relating to the assessment of teaching competence and knowledge also create obstacles to the improvement of teacher certification.

In recent years the teacher education and certification programs have been criticized. Levin (1980) has suggested the need to pay more attention to the outcomes of teacher education programs and

1. To specify educational outcomes or desirable teacher behaviors
2. To establish the value or social utility for these educational outcomes or teacher behaviors
3. To indicate those teacher characteristics that are related to valued student outcomes
4. To identify alternative methods for assuring the presence of appropriate teacher characteristics.

Whether or not this is possible is open to question. Teacher certification generally is required for teaching in public elementary and secondary schools. In many states, certification is not required of teachers in nonpublic elementary and secondary schools. Often no standards exist for teachers in schools serving children below the age of those enrolled in public schools. In addition, since child-care centers may not be considered schools, the requirements for teachers in those settings are not considered the responsibility of education authorities. Qualifications for those working in nursery schools and child-care centers are found in the licensing standards of state agencies that regulate those institutions. These standards establish qualifications for early childhood personnel that are generally lower than those for public school teachers.

Child-care personnel may include directors, teachers, and assistants. The director, the person with the highest status in a center, may only be required to have the equivalent of two years of post-secondary work with as few as 18 hours in child-related courses. Teachers and assistants may be expected to have even less formal preparation, and equivalences are established that allow practitioners to have a minimum level of academic preparation. When nursery schools are licensed as child-care centers, these qualifications apply to nursery school directors, teachers, and assistants as well.

The absence of certification standards for child-care workers and nursery school teachers that are equivalent to those for kindergarten and primary school teachers is probably rooted as much in economic interests as in academic ones. Child-care practitioners are the lowest-paid child welfare workers. Raising entry requirements for these practitioners would increase the pressure for higher pay and thus increase the cost of child-care service (Spodek & Saracho, 1982).

Credentialing

In the field of early childhood education, the Child Development Associate (CDA) credential was established to upgrade the qualifications of those who provide care for young children. To some extent, the CDA credential was designed to substitute for certification standards, which do not apply to nursery school and child-care staff. A system was developed for assessing the qualifications of child-care workers and for granting credentials to competent individuals.

Although the CDA credential is a national one, it is not a professional license to practice, nor is it recognized by all state teacher certification or child-care licensing agencies. The credential derives its authority from the requirement that practitioners in Head Start programs possess it. In addition, some states have used the credential as a means of documenting staff qualifications to meet day-care center licensing requirements.

To qualify for the credential, an individual must demonstrate competence in each of six areas:

1. To establish and maintain a safe, healthy learning environment
2. To advance physical and intellectual competence
3. To support social and emotional development and provide positive guidance
4. To establish positive and productive relationships with families
5. To insure a well-run, purposeful program responsive to participant needs
6. To maintain a commitment to the profession [CDA, National Credentialing Program, 1986, pp. 3–4]

In the original CDA credentialing system practitioners seeking the CDA credential would be evaluated based upon observed performance in working with children rather than through having completed a program of study at an institution of higher education. At present, some formal or informal training is required of those being assessed for credentialing.

An assessment team, consisting of the candidate, a trainer/advisor, a parent-community representative, and a CDA representative judge the candidate based upon performance rather than training. The candidate collects materials into a portfolio that best reflects her or his work with young children, parents, and center staff members. The candidate is observed in the classroom and is interviewed by the assessment team. Reports from the center staff on the individual's ability to work with young children, parents, and other staff members are also collected. A parent-community representative collects opinions about the candidate's work from other parents and also observes the candidate at work. In addition, an evaluator observes the candidate at work and interviews the candidate to clarify any issues that arise about her or his work. At an assessment meeting, those involved in the process assess the materials collected, the interviews, and the observations of the candidate's performance, to determine whether the candidate should be awarded the credential.

Over 16,000 CDA credentials have been awarded to date. While the original CDA consortium no longer exists, the credential continues to be offered by the Council for Early Childhood Professional Recognition, a unit of the NAEYC.

At the present time, the nature of early childhood teacher certification and credentialing seems to be in a state of flux in the United States. As more public schools offer educational programs to three- and four-year-olds, early childhood teacher certification standards are being established or modified in various states. Meanwhile, questions have been raised about the stability of the CDA credentialing system as well as its viability, as candidates are being expected to pick up an increasingly larger share of the cost of the assessment process. These forms of certification and credentialing have influenced the preparation of early childhood personnel as college and university programs feel the increased pressure to meet state certification guidelines and as community colleges modify their programs to allow graduates to meet the requirements of the CDA credential.

THE PREPARATION OF EARLY CHILDHOOD TEACHERS

The preparation of early childhood teachers is usually considered the domain of the four-year institution. While standards have been established for these programs by the National Council for the Accreditation of Teacher

Education (NCATE) and NAEYC, great variation can be found among programs. They usually include general education and professional education components. The professional education component consists of foundation courses, curriculum courses, methods courses, and teaching practice. Early childhood practitioners may also be prepared in two-year community and junior colleges, in vocational training centers, and in high schools. As requirements for early childhood practitioners vary greatly, so do training programs.

Early childhood teacher education programs are primarily housed in departments, schools, and colleges of education, with close ties to programs preparing elementary teachers. In the last two decades there have been many changes in these programs, with some having been newly established while others have been revised. Among the changes are additional required courses and changes in practica, in numbers of students enrolled, and in number and kind of faculty.

While some of these changes are attributable to a concern for accountability, many have been related to certification requirements demanding higher admission and retention standards (Spodek & Davis, 1982; Spodek, Davis, & Saracho, 1983). Standards for the approval of programs that prepare people for different teaching certificates are established within state departments of education. They tend to be heavily influenced by various educational constituencies, including local school boards, school administrators, teacher educators, and teachers' unions and associations. These same constituencies are represented by NCATE. While all these groups serve as gatekeepers to the teaching profession, teachers' unions and associations have asserted a growing influence over the preparation and certification of teachers. In the process, early childhood teacher education programs seem to be becoming more like other programs preparing teachers for other levels of education. As program development follows certification requirements, the conceptual nature of the program seems to be changing.

Perhaps there is a greater need today to have the organized field of early childhood education determine what constitutes competence in its practitioners as well as what conceptions of teaching are most appropriate for young children. Only by understanding what teachers do can we improve the preparation of teachers. Early childhood teacher education programs must become more responsive to the needs of working with young children. The guidelines for professionalism to be used should be responsive to early childhood education in particular.

One of the ways of increasing the level of professionalism of any field is to improve the quality of preparation required of its practitioners. This may occur in response to external forces, such as standards established by state licensing or certification agencies or reports of national commissions. However, analyzing practitioners and identifying characteristics that distinguish highly competent practitioners from less competent ones may also suggest change. It is expected that increased professionalism in early childhood education would result from the reform of early childhood teacher education.

REFORMING EARLY CHILDHOOD TEACHER EDUCATION

The preparation of all teachers has been significantly influenced by forces outside the field of education, as well as by those within the field. The greatest influence seems to have come from state teacher certification agencies. Current program requirements reflect a concern that early childhood teachers should be prepared to serve a wide range of clients. As a result, courses related to infancy, the handicapped, multiculturalism, and parenting have been added to programs. In addition, early childhood teachers are being prepared for a wide range of responsibilities, including working in child-care centers and administrating programs. Early childhood teachers are also being expected to be better educated and better prepared to teach.

In general, the composition of these courses and experiences is left to the discretion of the teacher education institutions. What is included is often based upon an institution's view of the attributes of good teachers and of how college programs can contribute to those attributes. Over the years, three categories of attributes of good teachers have been identified: (1) personal characteristics, (2) behaviors, and (3) knowledge and cognitive processes. Each of these will be discussed in turn.

Teachers' Personal Characteristics

Some of the earlier attempts to identify the attributes of good teachers focused on identifying personal characteristics related to good teaching. Almy and Snyder (1947), for example, suggested that teachers of young children should possess physical stamina, world-mindedness, an understanding of human development, a respect for personality, and a scientific spirit. Leeper (1968), following in the same tradition, suggested that teachers of young children should love children and that they should be kind, warm, outgoing, and secure and enjoy working with young children. Almy (1975) identified such attributes as a high energy level, patience, warmth, nurturance, openness to new ideas, a tolerance for ambiguity, flexible thinking, and maturity as qualities of a good early childhood teacher.

While such virtues are important for early childhood teachers, they have seldom been used as a basis for teacher education programs. Some of these teacher characteristics are related to personality attributes and are not very susceptible to change through college courses. Some, however, may be altered by training. One can, for example, improve a person's physical stamina through physical training, though such training is rarely included. Peters (1984) has suggested that, as early childhood teacher preparation, and specifically CDA training, leads to successful functioning in the field, it might influence a person's thinking and valuing. Saracho and Spodek (1983), in reviewing a broad range of collections of attributes for exemplary teachers, concluded that these collections often lack practical application in selecting or training teachers. They are seldom used as a basis for admission to training programs or for entrance to the profession. Thus, while there was a great deal of lip service given to reforming teacher education by selecting candidates with appropriate characteristics, little practical application was made of this concern for teachers with exemplary characteristics.

Teachers' Behaviors

More recently, attempts to identify the attributes of good teachers have focused on teachers' behaviors. This is reflected in studies of teacher performance and in the development of competency-based or performance-based teacher education programs. In such programs, statements of observable behaviors become the objectives of the program, and persons completing it are expected to demonstrate those performances at an acceptable level. Thus, the performance is more critical than the experience through which the performance is learned.

While performance-based evaluation was seen at first as an attractive approach to identifying the qualities of good early childhood teachers, the approach never achieved the expectations of its advocates. Taylor (1978) suggests that the competency-based movement is rooted more in the discourse of politics than of research, and he questions whether it is possible to identify specific teaching skills that represent functional teaching acts. Howey, Yarger, and Joyce (1978) suggest that, while the competency movement led to a restatement of goals, teacher education programs did not focus to any greater degree on how the behavior of teachers contributed to the goals' implementation. Perhaps the focus on teacher behavior has influenced how we discuss teaching more than how we train teachers.

Teachers' Knowledge and Cognitive Processes

The competency-based teacher education movement was based upon an analysis of teachers' observable performance. Competency was assessed by observing teachers in action and through task analysis or reflection. Saracho (1984) has suggested that a task analysis is inadequate for assessing what teachers do. Instead, she has proposed that a conceptual analysis of teaching be done. She identified the roles of early childhood teachers as

Decision makers. Teachers plan and create learning opportunities. The range of decisions they make relate to children, materials, activities, and goals.

Curriculum designers. Teachers develop a curriculum based upon the educational goals considered important by the community and the activities that are expected.

Organizers of instruction. Teachers assess learning needs, then organize classroom resources and activities relative to their educational goals.

Diagnosticians. Teachers develop information about their children's potential and limitations through observation and other assessment strategies, in order to provide the proper match between ability and opportunity.

Managers of learning. Teachers provide and maintain a learning environment that makes educational experiences accessible to children.

Counselor/advisors. Teachers assist individual children in acquiring desirable behaviors, in learning to deal with others, and in coping with their own feelings. Teachers instruct, coach, and model to achieve these ends.

These roles are directly related to the teacher's function within the classroom. When the role of the teacher is conceptualized beyond classroom responsibilities, other roles, such as child advocate, adult educator, or supervisor can be added.

The identification of the roles suggests that teacher performance requires more than observable skills or personal characteristics. Teachers of young children must acquire a range of knowledge, skills, and attitudes that are basic to the successful performance of each role.

A further analysis of teaching roles suggests that the decision making is not independent of the other roles. Rather, each role includes both a decision-making and a performance dimension. Teachers make immediate and reflex decisions, which are based upon judgments about the goals they want children to achieve, the characteristics of the children they teach, and the specific context in which they function. These professional judgments do not represent rule-following behavior, and, while they are imprecise, there is a consistency in the way that teachers function and in the decisions they make.

In essence, teachers are translating a set of theories into practice. The idea of theory underlying early childhood education practice is not novel, although the kinds of theory suggested have varied. Kohlberg and Mayer (1972) conceptualized ideologies in education that related to specific value orientations and development theories. Some early childhood educators (e.g., Caldwell, 1984) consider the field of early childhood education to be essentially the application of the science of child development. From this point of view, theories of child development translate directly into theories of early childhood teaching practice. A review of the literature of early childhood education over the years demonstrates that many early childhood programs reflected specific theories of child development. In the "Planned Variations Models" of Head Start, for example, each program model was characterized by the developmental theory in which it was grounded.

Just as early childhood education programs reflect ideologies and developmental theories, so do programs to prepare early childhood teachers. Spodek (1975) suggests that programs of teacher education be consistent with ideologies of the early childhood programs in which the teachers function. This suggestion is built upon an analysis of different forms of knowledge identified by Habermas (1971) and applied to early childhood education by Macdonald (1973). The three forms of knowledge identified were based upon: "(1) a technical cognitive interest in control, underlying the empirical analytic approach; (2) a practical cognitive interest in consensus underlying a hermaneutic-historical approach; and (3) a critical cognitive interest in emancipation or liberation underlying the self-reflective approach" (p. 2). The predominant approaches to early childhood education are rooted in technical control interests, whether they are concerned with cultural data (as in a behaviorist model) or with personal growth (as in an interactionist model) or with maturation (as in the romanticist model). None are rooted in emancipatory or practical interests (Spodek, 1975).

Seaver and Cartwright (1977), building upon this analysis, suggested that, rather than being matched to early childhood program ideologies, teacher education programs should foster ideological pluralism. Using Kohlberg and Mayer's (1972) work, they characterized different developmental theories as representing different ideologies and presented three different approaches to early childhood programs: the behaviorist, the interactionist, and the maturationist. In a sense, this ideological pluralism model reflects the child development tradition of early childhood education; however, when defined so narrowly as in these theories, it may be an inadequate basis for programs to prepare early childhood teachers. They do not make just technical decisions; they make moral ones as well. These moral decisions are based upon differing notions of the good, the true, and the beautiful, which cannot be derived from childhood development theory (Spodek, 1977).

The early childhood profession requires a broader foundation than that of technical knowledge. It must also find justification for practice in the realm of practical knowledge (Silin, 1985). The beliefs and theories that teachers develop about children, knowledge, and practice are a legitimate source of professional behavior, as important to early childhood education practice as the theories of developmental psychology.

In recent years, teachers' practical knowledge has been studied by a number of researchers (e.g., Bussis, Chittendon, & Amarel, 1976; Connelly & Clandinin, 1984; Elbaz, 1983; Halliwell, 1981; Silin, 1982; Spodek, 1987; Spodek & Rucinski, 1984). While the strategies used to identify teachers' practical knowledge vary among the studies, there is agreement that teachers themselves represent a source of knowledge about teaching and that teachers do generate legitimate theories and beliefs in relation to the practice of teaching.

In examining the thought processes of early childhood teachers, for example, Spodek (1987) identifies two distinct types of teacher thought: scientific concepts and value beliefs. Scientific concepts are related to the process of education and often seem to tie in with developmental theory or learning theory. Value beliefs, on the other hand, are concerned with the products of education, that is, what the teachers want the school program to do to or for children. These beliefs are based upon moral judgments or social expectations.

The teachers' value beliefs fall into 12 categories: goals for children's behavior, children's needs, classroom management, planning and organization, materials, learning and development, children's characteristics, instructional processes, educational play, academics, evaluation and assessment, and home and parents. Concepts and beliefs about classroom management, learning, children's characteristics, and instructional processes are among those most commonly held by teachers. This seems to suggest that the major interests of teachers rest in keeping children actively involved in classroom activities. Some concepts and beliefs are held in common by all or most teachers; others may be held by only a few or by a single teacher. These shared concepts and beliefs may constitute that part of a teacher's practical knowledge that represents the professional knowledge intersubjectively shared by all practitioners with common dispositions. It seems plausible, therefore, that a form of professional preparation could be developed that would be perceived as both theoretically sound and practical to classroom teachers.

SUMMARY AND CONCLUSION

Upgrading the level of professionalism among early childhood practitioners has led to a call for raising standards for practitioners. It has resulted in the establishment of a credentialing system and in the modification of teacher certification standards. The preparation of early childhood teachers is also changing: Additional courses are being required, and teaching practice is being modified.

While requiring prospective teachers to have more of what is already required might raise the level of professionalism for the field, it might be more useful to change early childhood teacher education programs to reflect what teachers actually do and why they do what they do. Studies of teachers' cognitive processes, the way teachers make decisions, and the theories and beliefs upon which their decisions are based can be coupled with studies of how teachers function in various settings. Such studies might lead to the identification of a core of practical professional knowledge growing out of early childhood education practice, which, when coupled with teachers' technical knowledge of developmental theory and learning theory, might improve and broaden the intellectual base for practice. Integrating these forms of knowledge within a teacher education program could help to increase the level of professionalism among the early childhood practitioners who emerge from these new programs.

REFERENCES

Ade, W. (1982). Professionalism and its implications for the field of early childhood education. *Young Children, 37*(3), 25–32.

Almy, M. C. (1975). *The early childhood educator at work*. New York: McGraw-Hill.

Almy, M. C., & Snyder, A. (1947). The staff and its preparation. In *Early childhood education, 46th yearbook of the National Society for the Study of Education* (Part 2) (pp. 224–246). Chicago: University of Chicago Press.

Bussis, A. M., Chittendon, E. A., & Amarel, M. (1976). *Beyond surface curriculum*. Boulder, CO: Westview Press.

Caldwell, B. (1984). From the president: Growth and development. *Young Children*, 39(6), 53–56.

Child Development Associate, National Credentialing Program. (1986). *Preschool caregivers in center-based programs*. Washington, DC: Council for Early Childhood Professional Recognition.

Connelly, F. M. & Clandinin, D. J. (1984). Personal practical knowledge at Bay Street School. In R. Halkes & J. K. Olson (Eds.), *Teacher thinking: A new perspective on persistent problems in education* (pp. 134–148). Lisse, Netherlands: Swets & Zeitlinger.

Elbaz, F. (1983). *Teacher thinking: A study of practical knowledge*. London: Croom Helm.

Greenwood, E. (1962). Attributes of a profession. In S. Nosow & W. H. Form (Eds.), *Man, work and society: A reader in the sociology of occupations* (pp. 207–218). New York: Basic Books.

Halliwell, G. (April, 1981). *Kindergarten teachers and curriculum construct systems*. Paper presented at the annual meeting of the American Educational Research Association, Los Angeles.

Howey, K. R., Yarger, S., & Joyce, B. (1978). Reflections on preservice preparation: Impressions from the national survey. *Journal of Teacher Education*, 29, 38–40.

Howsam, R. B., Corrigan, D. C., Denemark, G. W., & Nash, R. J. (1976). *Education as a profession*. Washington, DC: American Association of Colleges for Teacher Education.

Hughes, J. M., & Shultz, F. M. (1976). *Education in America* (4th ed.). New York: Harper & Row.

Kohlberg, L., & Mayer, R. (1972). Development as the aim of education. *Harvard Educational Review*, 42, 449–496.

Leeper, S. H. (1968). *Nursery school and kindergarten*. Washington, DC: National Education Association.

Levin, H. M. (1980). Teacher certification and the economics of information. *Educational Evaluation and Policy Analysis*, 2(4), 5–18.

Macdonald, J. B. (April, 1973). *Potential relations of human interests, language, and orientation to curriculum thinking*. Paper presented at the annual meeting of the American Educational Research Association, New Orleans.

National Association for the Education of Young Children. (1984). NAEYC position statement of nomenclature, salaries, benefits, and the status of the early childhood profession. *Young Children*, 40(1), 52–55.

Peters, D. L. (April, 1984). *Using performance/competence measures to determine readiness for professional entry in the field*. Paper presented at the annual conference of the National Association for the Education of Young Children, Los Angeles.

Saracho, O. N. (1984). Perception of the teaching process in early childhood education through role analysis. *Journal of the Association for the Study of Perception*, 19(1), 26–39.

Saracho, O. N., & Spodek, B. (1983). Preparing teachers for multicultural settings. In O. N. Saracho & B. Spodek (Eds.), *Understanding the multicultural experience in early childhood education* (pp. 125–146). Washington, DC: National Association for the Education of Young Children.

Seaver, J. S., & Cartwright, C. A. (1977). A pluralistic foundation for training early childhood professionals. *Curriculum Inquiry, 7*, 305–329.

Silin, J. (1982). *Protection and control: Early childhood teachers talk about authority*. Unpublished doctoral dissertation, Teachers College, Columbia University.

Silin, J. (1985). Authority as knowledge: A problem of professionalism. *Young Children, 40*(3), 41–46.

Spodek, B. (1972). Staff requirements in early childhood education. In I. J. Gordon (Ed.), *Early childhood education, 71st yearbook of the National Society for the Study of Education* (pp. 339–365). Chicago: University of Chicago Press.

Spodek, B. (1975). Early childhood education and teacher education: A search for consistency. *Young Children, 30*, 68–74.

Spodek, B. (1977). Curriculum construction in early childhood education. In B. Spodek & H. J. Walberg (Eds.), *Early childhood education: Issues and insights*. Berkeley, CA: McCutchan.

Spodek, B. (1987). Thought processes underlying preschool teachers' classroom decisions. *Early Child Development and Care, 28*, 197–208.

Spodek, B., & Davis, M. D. (1982). A study of programs to prepare early childhood personnel. *Journal of Teacher Education, 3*(2), 42–44.

Spodek, B., Davis, M. D., & Saracho, O. N. (1983). Early childhood teacher education and certification. *Journal of Teacher Education, 34*(5), 50–52.

Spodek, B., & Saracho, O. N. (1982). The preparation and credentialing of early childhood personnel. In B. Spodek (Ed.), *Handbook of research in early childhood education* (pp. 399–425). New York: Free Press.

Taylor, W. (1978). *Research and reform in teacher education*. Winsor, England: HFER Publishing.

6 • Where Is Early Childhood Education as a Profession?

LILIAN G. KATZ
University of Illinois

The purpose of this chapter is to examine some of the main characteristics of a profession and to apply them to the current state of the art of early childhood education. Most scholars of the subject of professions seem to agree that eight criteria must be met before an occupation may be classified as a profession (Freidson, 1986; Goode, 1983). In the absence of a formal or conceptual rationale for ordering the importance of the criteria, I shall introduce them in order of those to be treated most briefly first and most fully last.

SOCIAL NECESSITY

The work of a profession is essential to the functioning of a society; thus, the absence of its knowledge and techniques would weaken the society in some way (Becker, 1962; Larson, 1977).

The evidence bearing on whether or not the work of early childhood educators is essential to society is mixed at best. While recent reports of the longitudinal effects of early childhood education (Consortium, 1983) are encouraging, they need large-scale replication. We have yet to make a convincing case that teachers of the highest quality can provide to young children services without which society is at risk.

Given the power of later childhood and adolescent experiences to offset the benefits of good early ones, we must be careful in the statements we make about what we can achieve. We can be no more sure that the effects of good early experiences cannot be reversed than that early bad

This chapter is based on a paper presented to the ECHO Conference, Bristol Polytechnic, Bristol, England, September 20, 1985, in honor of E. Marianne Parry, O. B. E.

experiences can be remediated. Haskins's (1985) recent report of a long-term follow-up study of primary school children who had been in day care indicated that such children were more aggressive than children who had not been in day care and that those who had been in "cognitive" programs were more aggressive than those in other types of programs. These results are highly susceptible to misinterpretation and abuse by policy makers.

ALTRUISM

A profession is said to be altruistic in its motives. Ideally, professionals are expected to perform their services with unselfish dedication, if necessary working beyond normal hours and giving up personal comforts in the interests of society. On this criterion, early childhood education ought to be doing very well. Teachers of young children are not busy amassing riches or engaging in work that is easy or glamorous.

AUTONOMY

In most cases, a profession is an occupation that is autonomous in at least two ways (Forsyth & Danisiewicz, 1983). First, the client does not dictate to the practitioner what services are to be rendered. Second, professionals in large organizations or institutions are autonomous with respect to their employer, who also does not dictate the nature of practice but hires the professional to exercise judgment based on specialized knowledge, principles, and techniques. As Braude (1975) points out, "To the degree that a worker is constrained in the performance of his work by the controls and demands of others, that individual is less professional" (p. 105).

Issues concerning autonomy with respect to clients are far more complex. Early childhood educators have at least three client groups: parents, children, and the larger society or posterity. There is a paradoxical situation of our wanting to strengthen and increase parent involvement in their children's education, while at the same time wishing to exercise our autonomy as teachers. To develop as a profession requires that we learn how to respond to strident and often contradictory pressures in the light of our very best professional judgment, based on the best available knowledge and practices.

Most teachers think of children as their primary clients. A possible pitfall exists in this narrow view of the client group. Although children's preferences must be taken into consideration, decisions concerning teaching practices should not be made solely on the basis of the enjoyment of one client group. The appropriate goal for education—at every level—is to engage the learner's mind and to assist that mind in its efforts to make better and deeper sense of significant experiences. Enjoyment thus is a by-product rather than a goal of good teaching.

In a sense, society or posterity is the educator's ultimate client. But societies like ours often demand incompatible achievements. They want the young to learn to be both cooperative and competitive. They want conformity and initiative. It is no simple matter to help children learn where and when such different dispositions are appropriate. Our communities say that, at the least, they want excellence, high standards of achievement, and equality of opportunity. We must consider what principles of learning, development, and curriculum we can apply toward meeting such multiple and often contradictory expectations (Green, 1983).

CODE OF ETHICS

Professions subscribe to codes of ethics intended to protect the best interests of clients and to minimize yielding to the temptations inherent in the practice of the profession. In addition, professional societies institute procedures for disciplining members in cases of violations of the code of ethics (Katz, 1984c).

The development of a code of ethics for early childhood educators is not an easy task. The process involves identifying the major temptations confronted in the course of practice (Katz, 1984c). The code should address ethical dilemmas inherent in relations with children, parents, colleagues, employers, and the general lay public. Ethical norms of a group of colleagues, articulated in a code of ethics, can help to give individuals the feeling that colleagues will back them up when they take a risky but courageous stand in the face of an ethical dilemma.

The National Association for the Education of Young Children has formed a special commission to develop a code of ethics for its members. Several state branches of the association have already developed their own. Inasmuch as local values and cultural variations play a role in conceptions of ethical standards, it would seem wise for each country or cultural unit to develop its own. True professional status, however, requires a common code of ethics adopted by all practitioners within a given cultural or national community.

DISTANCE FROM THE CLIENT

Since, by definition, the practice of a profession requires bringing to bear a body of knowledge and principles to the solution of problems and predicaments, the relationship between practitioner and client is marked by optimum distance, disinterest, or "detached concern" (Katz, 1984a). This distance from the client is reflected in the strong taboo against physicians treating members of their own families, since emotional attachment might interfere with the exercise of reasoned judgment. This does not preclude such feelings as empathy or compassion but is intended to place them in appropriate perspective. Optimum distance is also expected to minimize the temptation to develop favorites and to inhibit the tendency to respond to clients in terms of personal predilection or impulses.

Many specialists and teachers in early childhood education resist this aspect of professionalism, and not without reason. They worry about meeting children's apparent need for closeness and affection. However, young children generally are capable of experiencing both feelings, even when the teacher maintains an optimum distance. Though effective teaching requires intimate knowledge of the pupils, this can be achieved by frequent contact, observation, and listening, without the emotionality required of family relationships. There is a stereotypical view of a professional as a remote, unresponsive, and intimidating expert who is likely to breed resentment among parents. To minimize such feelings on the part of parents, professionals have to learn how to achieve *optimum* warmth and responsiveness as well as optimum distance. This serves to protect the professional from the risks of emotional burnout, which can endanger the teacher's functioning as well as undermine her or his effectiveness with children. Optimum emotional distance permits the teacher to be responsive, caring, and compassionate, as well as to exercise professional judgment and bring knowledge to bear in responding to children.

STANDARDS OF PRACTICE

Professions adopt standards of practice that are significant in three ways:

1. The profession adopts standards below which it is hoped no practitioner will fall. Every practitioner applies standard procedures in the course of exercising professional judgment. In some measure these standards result in standardization of professional performance (i.e., all physicians follow standard procedures in making diagnoses, but exercise their own judgment in deciding what actions to take). In theory, at

least, professional practice is distinguished from the work of artisans, tradespersons, technicians, or bureaucrats in that it does not simply implement fixed routines, rules of thumb, or regulations. Rather than following a set of recipes, the professional practitioner acts on the basis of accepted principles that are taken into account in the formulation of professional judgment.

2. The standard procedures that are developed and adopted are addressed to the common predicaments that every member is expected to encounter fairly often in the course of practice, and these procedures are accumulated into the body of professional knowledge.

3. Professional standards of performance are universalistic rather than particularistic. This implies that all the knowledge, skill, insight, ingenuity, and so forth possessed by the practitioner is available to every client, independent of such irrelevant personal attributes of the client as social and ethnic background, ability to pay, or personal appeal.

One of the major tasks ahead for early childhood educators is to develop and articulate their perceptions of professional standards. We might begin by enumerating and describing the standard predicaments that all early childhood educators confront in the course of their day-to-day work. One such effort of my own (Katz, 1984a) depicts a situation in which four-year-olds quarrel over whose turn it is to use a tricycle. The responses of a professionally trained teacher are compared with the responses of an untrained person, in order to highlight how professional judgment can come into play.

PROLONGED TRAINING

A major defining attribute of a profession is that it requires entrants to undergo prolonged training. Although there are no standards by which to judge how long such training should be, the training process itself is thought to have several particular characteristics:

1. The training is specialized, in order to insure the acquisition of complex knowledge and techniques.

2. The training processes are difficult and require cognitive strain; thus, there will be a culling or screening process, and some candidates can be expected to fail. Training should be marked by optimum stress and sacrifice, resulting in dedication and commitment to the profession (Katz & Raths, 1985).

3. Candidates are required to master more knowledge than is likely to

be applied and more than the student perceives to be necessary. In all professions, candidates are said to complain about these excesses and the apparent irrelevance of much of the knowledge they are expected to master.

4. Institutions responsible for professional training must be accredited or licensed by processes monitored by practicing members of the profession. These institutions award certificates, diplomas, or degrees under the supervision of members of the profession.

5. All professional training institutions offer trainees a common core of knowledge and techniques so that the entire membership of the profession shares a common allusionary base.

6. Professional societies and training institutions, very often in concert, provide systematic and regular continuing education for members.

It is not clear what kind of training and how much of it is required for high-quality professional performance (see, for example, Katz, 1984b). We should stop being defensive about expecting candidates in teacher education to study theory, research, history, or philosophy. All professions expose their candidates to more knowledge than they ever apply, expecting not more than about a third of what is mastered to be retained. Furthermore, there is evidence to show that, even though one forgets facts and concepts once mastered, such knowledge enables one to go on absorbing new facts and concepts more easily, long after training has been completed (Broudy, 1983). In addition, there is a sense in which it is important for practitioners to be "literate" in their own fields. For example, although they may never use Montessori's ideas, all early childhood practitioners should know who she was and what ideas she espoused.

In many countries, there is cause for concern about the characteristics of entrants into training. Too often, young women are advised to enter into early childhood education because their shyness makes them unsuitable for work with older pupils or because they are not academically strong enough to take up a more challenging or profitable occupation. Sadly, we have heard anecdotal reports from several countries that preschool teachers have been urged to transfer into secondary teaching because they were judged "too good for infants."

Disheartening evidence also exists to suggest that, among graduates of teacher education degree programs, those with the greatest ability last the shortest length of time in the teaching service (Schlechty & Vance, 1981). As attractive alternative opportunities for women become available, this "brain drain" is likely to continue. It can only be stemmed if working conditions and pay scales are dramatically improved and if the needs of young children are given high social priority. To some extent, the field of early childhood education—especially day care—is caught in a vicious cycle: People enter it with few skills, and no one wants to pay good wages for workers with few skills. But, because the pay remains low, the likelihood is that those with little training and few skills will take up the work. How can we break this cycle? While we must acknowledge that there are poor teachers, even among those with extensive training, good inservice education can help. But what may be required for a real break in the cycle is public understanding and recognition of the potential benefits of high-quality education in the early years, and deeper public commitment to the welfare of young children.

It is not uncommon for laypersons to point out that they know of an outstanding teacher who had no training. Perhaps all of us can think of just such a gifted or "natural" teacher. This claim is, however, a dangerous one. Abraham Lincoln was a self-taught lawyer, but virtually everything about him was exceptional. Furthermore, there was a great deal less to be learned by lawyers in his time. A profession can never be designed on the basis of its exceptions. On the contrary, professional training is designed to provide *all* its practitioners with minimal standards to help them perform effectively. If all lawyers had Lincoln's remarkable qualities of mind and could teach themselves as thoroughly as he did, we might have no need for law schools.

SPECIALIZED KNOWLEDGE

A profession is an occupation whose practices are based on specialized knowledge, which is thought to have several characteristics:

1. The knowledge is abstract rather than concrete. As such it is unlike crafts, sports, trades, or bureaucracies, in which the knowledge may consist of rules of thumb, rules, or regulations.
2. The knowledge consists of principles that are reasonably reliable generalizations to be considered in the course of practicing the profession.
3. The knowledge underlying professional practice is organized into a systematic body of principles.
4. The knowledge and principles are relevant to practical rather than metaphysical or academic concerns. They are intended to rationalize the techniques of the profession and, as such, are oriented toward some kind of practical and socially useful end.
5. The body of knowledge is esoteric or exclusive in that it is known only to practitioners of the profession and is unknown to laypersons. In this

sense, the profession has a monopoly on most of its relevant knowledge and techniques.

6. Practitioners belong to professional societies that take responsibility for disseminating new knowledge relevant to practice by producing scholarly journals and by providing conferences and workshops through which members are kept informed.

It is not clear whether we can as yet identify the body of knowledge or some relevant set of reliable principles that may be used to forge an agreement regarding which are the best available practices in early childhood education. We each might begin by listing those principles we consider essential and worthy of inclusion, and then examining the list in a systematic way. To what extent would we agree with one another's lists? Finding answers to these questions is one of the biggest tasks ahead of us. Members of the early childhood education community, both as individuals and as members of a professional society, must come together to develop a consensus concerning the principles underlying our professional practice.

REFERENCES

Becker, H. S. (1962). The nature of a profession. In *Education for the professions: National Society for the Study of Education yearbook* (pp. 27–46). Chicago: National Society for the Study of Education.

Braude, L. (1975). *Works and workers: A sociological analysis.* New York: Praeger.

Broudy, H. S. (1983). The humanities and their uses: Proper claims and expectations. *Journal of Aesthetic Education, 17*(4), 125–148.

Consortium for Longitudinal Studies. (1983). *As the twig is bent.* Hillsdale, NJ: Lawrence Erlbaum Associates.

Forsyth, P. B., & Danisiewicz, T. J. (1983). Toward a theory of professionalization. In P. Silver (Ed), *Professionalism in educational administration* (pp. 39–45). Victoria, Australia: Deakin University Press.

Freidson, E. (1986). *Professional powers: A study of the institutionalization of formal knowledge.* Chicago: University of Chicago Press.

Goode, W. J. (1983). The theoretical limits of professionalism. In P. Silver (Ed.), *Professionalism in educational administration* (pp. 46–67). Victoria, Australia: Deakin University Press.

Green, T. F. (1983). Excellence, equity, and equality. In L. Shulman & G. Sykes (Eds.), *Handbook of teaching and policy* (pp. 318–334). New York: Longmans.

Haskins, R. (1985). Public school aggression in children with varying day-care experiences. *Child Development, 56,* 689–703.

Katz, L. G. (1984a). Contemporary perspectives on the roles of mothers and teachers. In L. G. Katz (Ed.), *More talks with teachers* (pp. 1–26). Urbana,

IL: ERIC Clearinghouse on Elementary and Early Childhood Education.

Katz, L. G. (1984b). The education of preprimary teachers. In L. G. Katz, P. J. Wagemaker, & K. Steiner (Eds.), *Current topics in early childhood education* (Vol. 5) (pp. 1–26). Norwood, NJ: Ablex.

Katz, L. G. (1984c). Ethical issues in working with young children. In L. G. Katz (Ed.), *More talks with teachers* (pp. 45–60). Urbana, IL: ERIC Clearinghouse on Elementary and Early Childhood Education.

Katz, L. G., & Raths, J. D. (1985, November–December). A framework for research on teacher education programs. *Journal of Teacher Education, 36*(6), 9–15.

Larson, M. S. (1977). *The rise of professionalism: A sociological analysis.* Berkeley, CA: University of California Press.

Schlechty, P. C., & Vance, V. S. (1981). Do academically able teachers leave education? The North Carolina case. *Phi Delta Kappan, 63*(2), 106–112.

7 • Gatekeepers to the Profession

MARTIN HABERMAN
University of Wisconsin-Milwaukee

DIRECT GATEKEEPERS

Expectations regarding how teacher licensure should work are understandably confused. In the 19th century it was common for teachers to be recommended by their school district superintendents for a state license. The school district employing the teacher examined his or her normal-school transcript, considered the teacher's on-the-job record, and in many cases even administered an examination covering various subject matters. The licensing agreement was among the state, the school district, and the teacher. In the first half of this century, as state requirements became delineated in terms of specific college courses, individuals completed state-specified college courses and then applied to the state. In some states, therefore, licensing became an agreement between the state and the individual aspirant who could prove she or he had completed the appropriate courses in any number of institutions. In other states, the school district remained involved as it had been in the 19th century, and an applicant needed a school superintendent to attest to a period of successful on-the-job teaching, in addition to having taken the required college courses.

Since World War II the trend moved to the establishment of approved university programs as the basis for licensure. This has changed the role of the university from a passive one of supplying individuals with courses they need for state licensure, to an active one in which the university and the state agree upon a program and the individual can only be licensed upon recommendation of the university. This is known as the *approved-program approach*, since individuals do not take single courses required by the state, but complete total university programs. This shift has concentrated power in the university, omitted the involvement of school superintendents in the licensing process, and placed the individual student at the discretion of the university.

In the last decade there has been an assault on the approved-program approach, as more and more states mandate what university programs should include. In addition, most states have instituted tests for assessing graduates and will no longer automatically license those who simply complete approved university programs. More recently, several states have reintroduced the concept of district-controlled licensure, in which the school district may recommend individuals directly to the state, with no university involvement whatever. This is called *alternative certification.*

Figure 1 presents a matrix diagram of what each constituency expects of the other. Even a cursory reading of this figure reveals the idealistic nature of what each expects of the other. The conceptual value of this figure is that it forces us to examine, in one place, the diversity and contradictory nature of these expectations.

There have never been sufficient numbers of prepared teachers in

Figure 1

EXPECTATIONS REGARDING TEACHER LICENSURE

	The State will	The University will	The Schools will	The Teachers will	The Public will
The *State* expects that		Accept and implement a system of increasing state control over its approved programs	Utilize only fully licensed teachers	All meet requirements for licensure and relicensure	See value in maintaining state control over university programs and individual teacher licensure
The *University* expects that	Disapprove low quality university programs		Utilize teachers as professional practitioners	Learn and use their university preparation in practice	Provide schools of education with necessary support
The *Schools* expect that	Permit the hiring of emergency and out-of-license teachers as needed	Be accountable for the performance of its graduates		Be effective in present forms of school organization	Support the recruitment and retention of the best prepared, most experienced teachers
The *Teachers* expect that	Institute license requirements that reflect what they need to know in practice	Educate and train them for success in the real world	Maintain conditions that enable them to teach successfully		Value their services and pay them as professionals
The *Public* expects that	Maintain license requirements that protect children and youth	Provide sufficient numbers of well-prepared teachers	Be accountable for the performance of its faculty	Be competent and accountable for pupils' learning at present salary levels	

the fields of math, science, foreign languages, and exceptional education. Periodically, there have also been shortages on various levels such as early childhood, elementary, and middle school. Since World War II there nearly always have been insufficient numbers of prepared teachers in most subject areas and at all grade levels in the major urban areas and in remote rural areas. The exceptions are the Great Depression prior to World War II and the period between 1975 and 1982, when RIFs (reductions in force) occurred in the major school districts (Currance, 1985; Edelfelt, 1986). Persistently, in all geographic areas, in all subject fields, and in all grades, large numbers of fully prepared teachers have resigned after only a brief attempt at teaching. Indeed, we can estimate that 50% of teachers leave within five years, and this turnover is undoubtedly greater in urban areas (Schlechty & Vance, 1981). As a result, the theory of how licensure should work has never conformed to the reality of providing enough teachers. As the saying goes, life is what happens to us while we're busy making plans.

School districts in urban and remote rural areas have always hired "emergency" teachers for classes they could not cover with fully prepared personnel. School districts have also utilized licensed teachers for classes out of their field. Texas is the most notable current example of these practices (Haberman, 1986).

The alternative approaches to licensure vary. In some instances the state directly tests and licenses individuals who are unaffiliated with a university teacher education program. In other instances the state empowers particular school districts to recruit and train individuals without professional on-the-job preparation. Since 1980 these developments have become known as "alternative certification programs." While many in the universities use this term, "alternative certification program" has now come to describe the practice of beginning teachers being recommended for state certification by a school district.

The foreseeable future will be a period that may be characterized by the conflicts between these two worlds of licensure. In the first world, the standards of pedagogic and university education will be intensified and extended. Only students with higher grade point averages who can meet higher standards of university performance will pass through the approved university programs. These students will also complete a fifth year or an on-the-job internship before they are licensed. The state will also require these students to pass competency exams prior to licensure. The university will base its more difficult, longer training on a professional knowledge base that is comparable to the standards of other university professional schools and also incorporates the methods of the best school practitioners. The proposals of the Holmes Group (1986) characterize these proposals.

In the second world of teacher licensure, the state will enable school districts to license individuals directly, with no pedagogic training. The state will be in the peculiar position of holding universities (and their students) to higher and higher standards of pedagogic and subject-matter education at the very same time it signals individuals and school districts that this body of knowledge does not exist or, if it exists, can be quickly picked up on the job. Figure 2 reflects the reality of the licensure compact and the conflicting sets of guidelines that the states will be administering.

Figure 2
THE FOUR-PARTY COMPACT OF TEACHER LICENSURE (In Reality)

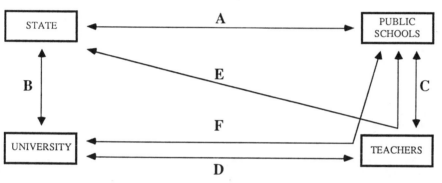

Agreement A   The state delegates to public schools the right to hire untrained teachers and to use out-of-license personnel in emergency situations. Public schools agree to provide on-the-job training that meets minimum state standards.

Agreement B   The state defines course content, passing scores for students on state exams and minimum standards for university programs. The university may only add to state requirements and agrees to offer programs.

Agreement C   Public schools hire untrained college graduates and provide on-the-job training. Teachers agree to complete training components offered by the school district.

Agreement D   Teachers may, as individuals, take courses or pursue degree programs offered by the university. The university deals with teachers who can be admitted to individual courses or to degree programs.

Agreement E   States administer tests for licensure directly to individuals who have not completed teacher education programs. Teachers agree to meet state standards for licensure as individuals working in one school district rather than as students in an approved university program.

Agreement F   Schools may require untrained teachers to take some university courses in addition to on-the-job training and inservice courses. Universities agree to provide district's untrained teachers with specific courses upon request.

INFORMAL GATEKEEPERS

Thus far we have discussed the direct gatekeepers—the state, the university, and the school districts—and argued that school districts and the state have tended to keep the gates more open than the universities have. In addition to these direct gatekeepers, however, there are informal ones which are of even greater importance. These are the parents, the early childhood profession, and those who choose to teach young children.

It must be stated that the great demand for more and better early childhood programs does not come primarily from a desire to improve the education of young children. Rather, it reflects contemporary social and economic conditions which require women to work. Working women have demanded and purchased day care, not early childhood education. This distinction is a significant one. It signals the difference between a program that is essentially benevolent and custodial and one that is developmental and educational. What parents perceive they want and what they can afford are frequently quite different from what experts in early childhood assert they should need and want. Since their primary need has been for the mother to be working, they do not seek to use all of her salary for day care. Indeed, the lower the cost of the custodial service, the better. The parents' goal in day care is that their children be kept physically safe, reasonably happy, and not be damaged or set back in any way. These are not educational goals and certainly not the goals of early childhood educators.

The indirect effect of such parental and societal expectations regarding day care leads logically and directly to the employment of individuals at minimum wage. Since day care is a minimum-wage operation, it serves as a very effective gatekeeper for the early childhood profession. What we have in operation, then, is the majority of working-class and middle-class women using day care for their own children in an effort to maintain a second or an only income. It is understandable that such economic pressure leads them to keep day-care costs down. Labor-intensive programs such as day care keep costs down by using few, if any, professionally prepared early childhood educators. Finally, and of equal importance, if such women are willing to use day care for their own children, it is highly unlikely that they would advocate that their tax dollars supply any more than custodial care for the children of the poor or disadvantaged, those on public assistance, or those who are institutionalized.

In the past 25 years, aspects of day care have become more sophisticated, incorporating better materials and differentiated staff so that some in attendance know something about the principles of child development, the use of materials, and curriculum. At the same time, many educational programs have become more like day care by extending the length of their programs and assuming custodial functions. There remains, however, a significant difference between programs whose primary goal is care and those whose primary goal is education. Unfortunately, it requires a high degree of sophistication for most people to discern the difference by simple observation.

In considering these indirect forces on licensure, the profession of early childhood education has itself served as an effective gatekeeper. While the motivation of the general public is essentially cost, the motivation of the professional is ostensibly quality—the quality of services that one wishes to offer to young children. In defining quality, the profession has aligned itself almost completely with the university-approved program approach (NAEYC, 1982). The National Association for the Education of Young Children has also developed guidelines and actually offers a Child Development Associate program. A few universities and many community and junior colleges focus on programs of one or two years. The numerous "excellence-in-education" reports documenting declines in literacy are pressuring universities to lengthen their teacher education programs and move them into the graduate levels, not to shorten such programs and make them available to nonuniversity populations.

The definition of early childhood as spanning the ages from birth through eight means, in effect, that those who might be interested in teaching in kindergarten or the first three grades will go to the university, but those who will be working with children younger than four will be employed in day-care centers at minimum wage. Those who choose to work with very young children would be foolish to spend a minimum of four years learning a complex profession which they could enter as high school graduates or with a year or two at a community college.

In this way, the parents' expectations for day care, the profession's insistence on a university-approved program for initial certification, and the future teacher's unwillingness to become a professional who works for minimum wage all combine to serve as very effective indirect gatekeepers. There is no good reason to expect the recruitment of more able teachers for young children below age four or five (in nonpublic school settings), if each of these constituencies maintains its present advocacy.

Self-selection is the most powerful force in any occupational recruitment. Those who voluntarily seek to enter and be trained in a field are likely to be predisposed, by inclination and experience, to succeed. By far the largest population of individuals who are most interested in early childhood (birth to five years of age) are not college-age youth but experienced mothers. The university requirements—especially the time schedules, the costs, and the academic standards—effectively screen this population out, although many of these individuals have served as aides and volunteers in day-care centers. (Several institutions, with long histories in early childhood and in urban education, are exceptions to this general condition.)

It is curious that it is the university's general studies requirements that serve as the gatekeeper for this population. Many of them cannot enter schools or departments of education directly, where it is likely that they would earn passing grades and be certified, since they have not completed the required general or liberal arts studies. In most first-order universities these courses take approximately two years of full-time study and are the prerequisites for entrance into an early childhood education program. This situation is especially obvious in relation to minority mothers who serve as aides, who have raised large families, and who have completed some sort of child-care program at a community college. Every institution "wants" them, but somehow few are admitted. The gatekeeper is not the professional education of the university per se, but the liberal studies of the university. I use the term "curious" to describe this situation, since I have never heard an early childhood expert, researcher, or teacher who attributed her or his success to the liberal studies courses taken as freshmen and sophomores. Early childhood educators have proven to be quite effective gatekeepers over licensure, but in the process have given the education of young children over to those who run day care.

Within the world of the university, the problems deal with less important stakes. Preparation programs are aimed at future teachers who will work with children ages five through eight in school settings. They will have little impact on the majority of young children below age five in nonschool settings, whose need for education is infinitely greater. In addition, university programs are further limited by not preparing the kindergarten and primary teachers for urban school districts, but focusing instead on the teachers of small-town, rural, and suburban districts. Considering the demographics of the situation, the indirect gatekeeping has been so effective that the issue of who controls approved university programs directly remains a tepid concern at best. We are left with issues such as, Does the state or the university decide how much field experience is required? Does the state or the university decide on the test to be used for licensure of the graduates? Are future early childhood teachers prepared as mere reading teachers and skills teachers, or as child development specialists? These are currently the chestnut issues of early childhood education, which no longer bear any relation to reality.

The present situation places most state departments of education in direct control over the courses and general content in most university programs. The graduates hired into school districts are expected to prepare children for success as operationally defined in schools, that is, success in subsequent grades and on standardized achievement tests.

The issue of who is teaching the masses of these youngsters in urban school districts and before the age of five has nothing to do with university-approved programs or the accreditation of university programs. This is not to imply that education for children ages five through eight in nonurban settings is unimportant. It is of great importance, but nonurban children are not generally disadvantaged. Disadvantaged may be defined as the degree to which a child is dependent on an educational program for his or her essential developmental life experiences.

CONCLUSION

The primary contention of this chapter has been that the special nature of educating *all* children from birth to age five and *urban* children from birth to age eight has led to two sets of indirect gatekeeping functions: The first keeps potentially able teachers out of early childhood programs; the second keeps early childhood teachers/educators away from the programs offered for the overwhelming majority of young children in America.

Professors of education, who number approximately 45,000 in the United States, include many subsets of specialists who have made themselves irrelevant to practice, to varying degrees, by virtue of becoming institutionalized in universities. In no case, however, is the dislocation between the field—as practiced—and the expertise—as professed—as great as it is in early childhood education.

REFERENCES

Currance, C. (1985, September 5). Shortages of '85 vanish as schools hire uncertified teachers. *Education Week*, pp. 1, 11.

Edelfelt, R. (1986, Summer). Managing teacher supply and demand. *Action, 5,* 31–36.

Haberman, M. (1986, Summer). Alternative teacher certification programs. *Action, 5,* 13–18.

Holmes Group. (1986). *Tomorrow's Teacher.* East Lansing, MI: The Holmes Group Inc., 501 Erickson Hall, East Lansing, MI 48824.

Kagen, S. L. (1985, December 11). Four-year-olds and the schools. *Education Week*, pp. 4–5.

Martin, A. (1985). Back to kindergarten basics. *Harvard Educational Review.* 55, 310–320.

National Association for the Education of Young Children. (1982). *Early childhood teacher education guidelines.* Washington, DC: NAEYC.

Schlechty, P. C., & Vance, V. S. (1981). Do academically able teachers leave education? The North Carolina case. *Phi Delta Kappan, 63*(2), 106–112.

8 • The Child Development Associate Credential and the Educationally Disenfranchised

DONALD L. PETERS
University of Delaware

Calling oneself or one's occupation "professional" does not make it so. One has to be viewed as a professional both by oneself and by others. Recognition as a professional has two meanings which may or may not coincide. First, the meaning of the term focuses attention toward the character of the behavior of the individual who wishes to be called professional. Acting professionally means acting autonomously, rationally, and ethically in the exercise of one's knowledge and skills. Behaving professionally implies both freedom and responsibility. Second, the term is used to represent a person who holds membership in an occupation that is recognized as professional, that is, it has the prerequisite organization, structure, and entry control. This implies public recognition.

Both definitions stress the notion of "internal locus of control." The professional as an individual is self-motivated, self-directed, and self-confident. The professional has freedom of choice and the capability to make decisions for which she or he may be held accountable. A profession, as a collective, has control over its own destiny and that of its members. In both cases such freedom and control bring with it both tangible (e.g., money) and intangible (e.g., respect) rewards. Obtaining such rewards, however, requires access to the profession and public awareness and appreciation of the professional's exercise of freedom and responsibility.

The intent of this chapter is to review the Child Development Associate National Credentialing Program and its role in gaining public recognition for the professionalism of those who have been educationally disenfranchised in U.S. society. Suggestions also are offered as to why the CDA credential falls far short in establishing a profession in the organizational sense.

EVOLUTION OF THE CHILD DEVELOPMENT
ASSOCIATE NATIONAL CREDENTIALING PROGRAM

From its inception in 1965, Head Start represented a commitment not only to low-income children and their families, but to low-income community residents more generally. The program was geared toward hiring "indigenous nonprofessionals" and providing them with both educational opportunities and a career development ladder that would provide the necessary access to professional status. The federal government, through the Office of Child Development (OCD), initiated during the late 1960s and early 70s a series of efforts that included inservice training, Head Start Supplementary Training (HSST) (college training leading to a certificate, A.A., or bachelor's degree), and Child Development Associate (CDA) training.

While responsibility for the training remained with OCD, a separate procedure was established for the credentialing process. In the hope of promoting rapid and wide acceptance of the new credential, a consortium was formed, consisting of representatives of 39 national associations that had direct interest in early childhood education and child development. Members of the consortium defined and approved the competency domains and functional areas to be covered by the credential, as well as piloted and implemented the assessment and credentialing procedures. Their efforts were almost entirely funded by federal money. (For a more thorough review of the history of the issues surrounding CDA, see Peters, 1981; Trickett, 1979. For a review of the research on CDA training, see Peters & Benham, in press).

Whereas the HSST training funded by federal funds represents a traditional route for education and professional improvement, the Child Development Associate Credentialing Program is unique and innovative. It represents an important case example for highlighting the critical issues in training and credentialing "professionals." Its uniqueness derives from the following facts:

1. It was initiated with the explicit intent and purpose of assessing and gaining public recognition for competency in working with young children and for establishing a new category of professional.
2. It was initiated and funded by the federal government.
3. It began as a full-blown national effort endorsed by and involving a wide range of other professions (e.g., American Psychological Association, American Association of Elementary, Kindergarten and Nursery Educators).

4. The program bypassed all existing local and state regulatory agencies and institutions of higher education.
5. It was specifically designed to meet the needs of the poor and educationally disenfranchised—those who would not otherwise have access to "professional" status through normal educational routes.

In other words, the CDA effort represented a direct and relatively well-funded attempt to establish professionalism and professional status in early childhood education, in one concerted effort, while bypassing the usual educational, licensure, and accreditation channels.

While an assault on the existing system, the CDA training and credentialing processes have certainly remained true to the original intent of serving primarily the previously educationally disenfranchised. A number of research studies and surveys have confirmed that the bulk of CDA trainees and credential recipients are women in their mid-thirties, who have as their highest educational attainment the high school diploma. They represent a mix of ethnic backgrounds, geographical locations, and employment settings. They are frequently parents themselves, and the vast majority come from low-income situations (Granger, Lombardi, & Gleason, 1984).

Assessment of the successes and failures of the effort to establish the CDA as a professionally recognized credential can be very instructive as the movement toward professionalism continues. The analysis provided derives from an exploration of the interplay of the two levels of meaning of the word *professional*, with which this discussion began.

BEHAVIORAL REQUIREMENTS
OF EARLY CHILDHOOD SETTINGS

The literature on professionalism suggests two characteristics of professional behavior, related to the issues of freedom and responsibility. True professionals, the literature suggests, act in ways that reflect client autonomy and organizational autonomy. The former refers to the ability to make decisions that affect the client without direct consultation with or agreement by the client. Such decisions, of course, are based upon one's special knowledge or expertise. Organizational autonomy refers to the individual's capability to act independently and with professional freedom within an employing organization and to be responsible for one's actions.

These characteristics of professionalism can be contrasted with those ascribed to early childhood personnel in the early education literature.

Almy (1975), for example, included such characteristics as high energy level, patience, warmth, nurturance, openness to new ideas, tolerance for ambiguity, flexibility of thought, and personal maturity. Others would add a positive self-concept, positive attitudes and expectations toward children's achievement, a thorough understanding of child development, and the ability to translate knowledge about child growth and development into a consistent pattern of behavior (Combs, 1965; Peters, 1984; Spodek, Saracho, & Lee, 1984). These characteristics focus our attention on the teacher's knowledge base, attitudes, and practical problem-solving abilities, and the ability to use these in service to the client. The knowledge, attitudes, and abilities represent an internalized expertise that permits autonomous action.

The necessity for internalized expertise makes a great deal of sense when considered within the context of the setting in which early childhood educators work. Four characteristics of that context seem particularly important: the autonomy of the organizational structure, the diversity of the clientele, the social complexity of the working environment, and the relative isolation from other colleagues.

Organizational Autonomy

Until recently, early childhood education settings have traditionally operated autonomously, almost always outside the mainstream of public education, and usually with minimal regulation of program content or curriculum. The field has prided itself on this organizational autonomy and has fought to retain it (Caldwell, 1981).

Curricula have been based upon a range of developmental and learning theories or educational philosophies (Peters, Neisworth, & Yawkey, 1985). The decision for their selection, rejection, or adaptation usually has been left up to individual teachers, education coordinators, or program directors. Within most programs enrolling children under five, staff members design and implement their own ideas or borrow freely from each other. Indeed, federal programs have encouraged or mandated locally designed options and have stressed individualization. Further, since most of the programs are relatively small and have no formal links to other programs, the great majority of overall planning and virtually all daily planning is carried out at the level of the individual group or classroom. Parents are often consulted in this planning, but the expectation is that the teacher has the knowledge and skills needed to lead the process and guarantee its developmental appropriateness.

The level of program autonomy—client and organizational autonomy—present in the early childhood field gives the teacher a range of latitude and freedom that greatly exceeds that experienced by most public school teachers. It follows that early childhood teachers must be able to plan and carry out their own programs, select their teaching methods, and organize materials and environments to meet the needs of diverse children; and they must do so in a consistent, positive, and effective manner.

Client Diversity

Developmental variability among children is great during the early childhood years, even within a fairly narrow chronological age span. Public Law 94–142 (the Education for All Handicapped Children Act), with its recent revisions and the mandated inclusion of handicapped children within Head Start classes, has further increased the heterogeneity in most programs. Yet the goals and curricula in early childhood education have not traditionally been limited to the academic subject-matter areas. Early childhood personnel have historically taken responsibility for the development of the "whole child," and in many cases the whole family. This increases markedly the need for individual decision-making and problem-solving skills and for the constant exercise of "professional" judgment.

Social Complexity

Early childhood teachers work more directly with adults than do most teachers of older children. Most center-based early childhood programs have more than one adult per classroom, and the role of the teacher usually includes responsibility for training and supervision. In addition, early childhood teachers work more closely with parents than do teachers at other levels of education. The interpersonal relationships among staff, children, and parents can often become quite complex.

Isolation

The organizational autonomy of early childhood programs also often leads to the isolation of the individual teacher from colleagues of similar background and training. Early childhood educators must be motivated to seek out their own opportunities for keeping current or abreast of changes in the field. As is the case for many autonomous professionals, teachers must use individual initiative to read journals or periodicals, to attend meetings of professional organizations, or to seek further education.

Taken together, these characteristics of the early childhood education setting require that effective teachers behave in a planful, flexible, independent manner based upon firmly grounded attitudes, beliefs, and knowledge about child development and learning. They must continuously exercise professional judgment and engage in independent problem solving, to meet their own needs and those of a complex and diverse clientele.

These behaviors sound very much like those suggested by the literature on professionalism.

THE CDA CREDENTIAL AS A
TEST OF PROFESSIONAL BEHAVIOR

Basic to the CDA credentialing system is the notion that it is possible to assess the degree to which an individual, functioning within an early childhood setting, possesses the underlying qualities of an effective teacher. The assumption is that these qualities will be reflected in observable behavior. This assumption is no different for the CDA credentialing process than it is for any other measurement system that attempts to provide judgments of hypothetical constructs. The requirements for validation of the linkage between the constructs and the observed behavior are the same.

Clearly, the CDA competencies represent what a broad array of experts, educators, and practitioners deem to be important behaviors for early childhood personnel. That is, the CDA behavioral competencies as observed in the classroom and documented in the portfolio, by the nature of the way they were formulated, have content validity. There is also some literature on other forms of validity, particularly concurrent and predictive validity, which reports on research conducted by those not directly involved in the original consortium efforts or in the day-to-day operation of the credentialing program. While such literature is limited, it is supportive of the CDA credential as an indicator of "professional" performance as it has been defined here.

The basic concept behind the CDA credentialing system is viable if and only if the level of competency—the configuration of the behaviors observed—is the correct one. The indicators to be sought are those that demonstrate the constructs of self-directedness, planfulness, knowledge, flexibility, social and communication skills, and self-confidence. There are some data to suggest that the indicators in the CDA process do get at these constructs. For example, Ruopp, Travers, Glantz, and Coelen (1979), in their study of day-care programs, used a 235-item observation instrument based upon the original 13 CDA functional areas. They factor-analyzed the observation results and found the check sheet yielded a global competency score and four subscores (Resources, Environment, Classroom Management, and Child Orientation) that were found to relate significantly to children's test-score gains.

Similarly, recently published research results suggest that training for CDA competencies produces in the candidate an increased knowledge of child development, more positive attitudes toward children's learning, stronger and more coherent beliefs in a child-centered approach toward early education, an increase in educational aspirations and further professional development, more active seeking of educational opportunities, and an increased sense of self-confidence in one's abilities to handle the complexity of the job (Peters & Benham, 1987; Peters & Sutton, 1984).

While there is a need for continuing validation research, the evidence to date is at least as strong as that available for any other teaching credentialing system. Further, there are at least some data to support the notion that CDA trained teachers are not different from those trained through a more traditional four-year certification program, on some measured variables (Peters & Sutton, 1984), and may be more effective in working with low-income parents. Such data should not be overinterpreted, but they again point to the validity of the multimeasure, multijudgment CDA credentialing system for assessing the attributes and competencies of effective, "professional" teachers.

THE PROFESSION

Several criteria for defining a profession seem to be generally agreed upon (cf. Austin, 1981; Keith-Lucus, 1980; or other chapters within this volume). Three are the focus of this discussion: controlled entry, a shared knowledge base, and self-regulation.

Controlled Entry

Controlled entry means that licensure, certification, and competency standards are in command of the profession itself rather than in the hands of external regulatory bodies. Implied in this statement is the notion that there is a consensually agreed-upon competency standard and a measurement system for assessing it.

Although consultation and advice are sometimes sought from the early childhood community, credentialing, teacher certification, and teacher education program accreditation standards across the United States usually reside in one or more state governmental agencies. Across state boundaries, or even within a single state, standards often vary widely for persons doing essentially the same job (Peters, Cohen, & McNichol, 1974). Currently there is no consensual agreement upon standards or their assessment.

The CDA competencies have received some level of support within day care and Head Start, but are little recognized in other sectors of early education. Although it has aimed to be a national standard, the CDA credential is accepted only in some 37 states and, even then, only for some early childhood positions, usually those below the "professional" level. The NAEYC, the largest professional organization in the early childhood education field, has now taken responsibility for CDA assessment and credentialing. As a result, there is potential for the first time for the CDA becoming a nationally accepted, competency-based system endorsed and controlled by the profession itself. Yet, within NAEYC itself, the tensions are great between constituencies favoring four-year degrees, two-year degrees, or the CDA.

The CDA credential is available for center-based personnel, home visitors, family day-care providers, and those who work in bilingual situations or with infants or handicapped children. Hence, it has the potential for providing unity across disparate portions of the early childhood arena. It lacks acceptability, however, within areas usually covered by public school certification requirements and therefore continues the disenfranchisement of some portions of the population.

Shared Knowledge Base

The second criterion for a profession requires that it define an identifiably unique, common educational knowledge base and set of skills that adequately represent the expertise of the field. Related to this are the notions that the profession can (1) generate new knowledge necessary to advance the field, (2) assume the major responsibility for the transmission of that knowledge to neophyte members, and (3) define the relationship between possession of the desired knowledge and skill and the criteria for entrance into the profession.

Although notable attempts at defining the knowledge base for the early childhood field have appeared, most have been set forth as program or curriculum guidelines and remain relatively nonspecific. They have remained so as a pragmatic acknowledgment of the constraints involved in meeting the needs of many different institutions, and as an acknowledgment of basic differences in beliefs of members of a multidisciplinary and varied field. The complex history and evolution of the field—with its roots in social work, education, pediatrics, child development, and several other disciplines—make consensual agreement difficult at best.

The CDA credentialing process is mute on this issue. No specific "knowledge" test is required; indeed, this has been one of the major criticisms of the process (Berk & Berson, 1981). Similarly, the only federal guidelines for CDA training programs are directed at the process, rather than the content, of the training. No required knowledge base is specified. This being the case, the three related issues noted earlier become largely irrelevant.

Self-Regulation

Although closely related to the two previous criteria of a profession, self-regulation goes beyond entry and educational control. There must be an ongoing evaluation process for continuously monitoring professional performance. It requires (1) a set of ethical standards and basic operating procedures against which member performance can be measured and (2) the availability of meaningful sanctions for self-policing.

Ethical standards are being discussed within the NAEYC, and surveys have been done of the membership; thus, it is likely that a set of standards will emerge. Whether these will apply to all members, whether they will be applicable to CDAs, or whether they will be accompanied by any meaningful sanctions is not clear. At any rate, at the present time, they are nonexistent.

While continuing education for early childhood teachers is required in some states for maintenance of certification, it is often nonspecific and certainly not universal. Maintenance of the CDA credential does require periodic update of materials but does not require a complete, standardized reassessment.

In sum, the early childhood field as a whole, and the CDA credentialing and training program in particular, fall far short on the generally accepted criteria for defining a profession.

CONCLUSION

This brief review of the CDA training and credentialing efforts of the last 15 years is instructive for those who are active in the movement toward professionalism of the early childhood education field. The data from several studies indicate that the CDA program has provided the previously or otherwise educationally disenfranchised with a means of becoming credentialed. Over 20,000 such credentials have been issued, and the credential has gained relatively wide recognition within state regulations of early education and child care. There is evidence that the credential—or, more accurately, the training that prepares the individual for assessment—has promoted behaviors that are rightly acknowledged as professional. Through newsletters, CDA Days at the NAEYC, and other means, a sense of professionalism has been fostered within a group that otherwise might not have shared such feelings.

There are also some data from follow-up studies of CDAs that indicate that receiving the credential provided opportunities for advancement in employment (Granger, Lombardi, & Gleason, 1984). At least some of the educationally disenfranchised, "indigenous nonprofessionals" have ended up in higher-prestige and higher-paying teaching and administrative positions, but the percentage is relatively small and the majority of persons receiving the credential report few promotions and little in the way of increased pay (Peters & Sutton, 1984). When such advancement is noted it appears to be more closely related to educational accomplishments than to the credentialing itself (Pettygrove, 1981).

It seems, therefore, that the successes of the CDA as a major federally funded innovation have more to do with increasing professionalism or professional behavior than with establishing a profession. Further, it is the latter that appears to carry with it the majority of tangible and intangible rewards that come with public acknowledgment and respect.

This conclusion is not surprising in some ways. The CDA program, by bypassing existing, publicly acknowledged structures and institutions, set itself apart from the mainstream of the educational establishment and rejected, at least in part, one of the principal "currencies" of success in the marketplace—academic credits and degrees. In place of that currency it offered a new one—the CDA credential—with uncertain backing or redemption value. Efforts toward establishing the redemption value, via validation studies whose results could be promulgated both within the early education community and with the general public, have been too few.

In creating a new vehicle for the poor and educationally disenfranchised, it was assumed that the road toward professional status would be opened. However, the new vehicle was created without explicit concern for some of the major components that are needed for building a profession. In particular, missing is a commitment to an explicit knowledge base upon which practice may be based. Further, in a field that is struggling on many fronts to receive proper acknowledgment for its unique contribution and skills, the concept of alternative entries into the profession is itself threatening. If two controlled entries are permitted, and one of them does not follow the usual pattern set by other professions, why not have three or four means of entry? Or, to the outsider, the more logical question may be, why have any? To state that the main route is biased against the poor and minorities does not completely satisfy. Head Start Supplementary Training and affirmative action programs that offer compensation through traditional routes seem more likely to be accepted and rewarded by the public and are less threatening to the mainstream of the field. To the extent that the CDA program attracts the educationally disenfranchised into training programs, encourages them to seek further education, and launches them into more traditional educational programs, it serves a similar purpose; however, the CDA credential then becomes but one marker along the route toward full professional status, which still must come from the traditional educational routes.

REFERENCES

Almy, M. (1975). *The early childhood educator at work*. New York: McGraw-Hill.

Austin, D. (1981). Some observations on the dismal state of the education of child care workers. *Child Care Quarterly, 10*(3), 250–260.

Berk. L. E., & Berson, M. (1981). A review of the Child Development Associate credential. *Child Care Quarterly, 10*(1), 9–42.

Caldwell, B. (1981). Day care and the schools. *Theory Into Practice, 20*(2), 121–129.

Combs, A. W. (1965). *The professional education of teachers: A perceptual view of teacher preparation*. Boston: Allyn and Bacon.

Granger, R., Lombardi, S., & Gleason, D. (1984, April). *The impact of the Child Development Associate program on CDAs*. Paper presented at the annual meeting of the American Educational Research Association, New Orleans.

Keith-Lucas, A. (1980). On being truly professional. *Child Care Quarterly, 9*(4), 243–250.

Peters, D. L. (1981). New methods for educating and credentialing professionals in child care. *Child Care Quarterly, 1*(1), 3–8.

Peters, D. L. (1984). *Introductory skills program for child services personnel (CDA training: Description and evaluation)*. University Park: The Pennsylvania State University, College of Human Development.

Peters, D. L., & Benham, N. (in press). Research on child development associate training. In S. Kilmer (Ed.), *Advances in day care and early education*. Greenwich, CT: JAI Press.

Peters, D. L., Cohen, A. S., & McNichol, M. (1974). The training and certification of early childhood personnel. *Child Care Quarterly, 3*, 39–53.

Peters, D. L., Neisworth, J. T., & Yawkey, T. D. (1985). *Early childhood education: From theory to practice*. Monterey, CA: Brooks/Cole.

Peters, D. L., & Sutton, R. E. (1984). The effects of CDA training on the beliefs, attitudes, and behaviors of Head Start personnel. *Child Care Quarterly, 13*(4), 13–17.

Pettygrove, W. (1981). The Child Development Associate credential as a child care staff standard. *Child Care Quarterly, 10*(1), 43–58.

Ruopp, R., Travers, J., Glantz, F., & Coelen, C. (1979). *Children at the center* (Vol. 1, Final Report for the National Day Care Study). Cambridge, MA: ABT Associates.

Spodek, B., Saracho, O., & Lee, R. (1984). *Mainstreaming young children.* Belmont, CA: Wadsworth.

Trickett, P. (1979). Career development in Head Start. In E. Zigler & J. Valentine (Eds.), *Project Head Start* (pp. 315–338). New York: Free Press.

9 • Men in Early Childhood Education

KELVIN SEIFERT
University of Manitoba

Traditionally, men have constituted only a small part of all early childhood educators. In 1984, for example, somewhere between 1 and 3 million persons defined themselves as direct child-care providers or early childhood educators of some type (NAEYC, 1985), but only about 5% of these were male. Early childhood education as a profession therefore includes somewhere between 50,000 and 150,000 male practitioners (U.S. Bureau of the Census, 1985). This makes men in this field about as common, for example, as doctors in family practice.

Yet men have an importance to this field beyond their small numbers. Their very absence has limited what early childhood educators can know about male practitioners directly; that is, we must often rely on impressions of men in other situations or jobs. Their absence may also have affected salaries and working conditions, probably for the worse. Even professional attitudes may have been defined too narrowly as a result of the one-gender history of early childhood education. But of this, more later.

These comments imply several reasons why men in early childhood education may be scarce. The rest of this chapter will make these more explicit. In brief, it will argue that men do not avoid early childhood education because they lack commitment or caring for young children. On the contrary, their behavior in another role—as fathers—suggests a large reservoir of positive personal interest in children. Rather, men are scarce because economic conditions in early childhood education are poor and because early childhood educators themselves do not fully understand what males can and cannot contribute to this field by virtue of their gender. Explicit discrimination against males in early childhood education is rare, certainly less common than among female minorities who enter male-dominated occupations.

POTENTIAL FOR MALE INTERACTION
WITH YOUNG CHILDREN

Compared to their scarcity in early childhood education, males seem relatively involved with young children as parents, though they still spend less time with children than do women. The difference between male and female parents is not as large as often believed, and in any case it does not seem to reflect differences in the feelings that men have for children.

Time Commitment

Fathers spend an average of 15 to 25 minutes per day in focused interaction with their children, and an average of 2 to 3.5 hours per day in activities that involve children only partially or intermittently (Hoffman, 1984; Pleck, 1983). These amounts all tend to be higher with fathers of preschoolers and decrease as the children get older. They have not changed over the last two or three decades.

The amounts may be lower than some people prefer, but they are not as low as popular stereotypes sometimes imply. In the past 30 years, in fact, fathers have increased their *proportionate* contribution to child care significantly, partly because mothers—including even those who do not work outside the home—have decreased the absolute amount of time they spend on child care and housework, during this same period. Not surprisingly, mothers who do work outside the home have decreased the time they give to child care and housework even more. In the late 1970s, as a result, fathers in two-career families were doing about one-third of the total child care, broadly defined (Pleck, 1983). In one-career families, they did only about one-sixth of the total child-care work. The figures vary a bit among studies and according to whether the data were collected via diaries, interviews, or observations (Pleck, 1985; Kimmel, 1987). In general, they are roughly consistent.

Psychological Involvement

Given that fathers spend less time with children than do mothers, do they also feel less psychological involvement with their children and families? Here, too, research contradicts common stereotypes: It consistently suggests that both sexes care more about their families than about their work and that the sexes do not differ much in this regard. For example, both sexes report thinking about their children while at work, much more often than they think about work while at home. And both sexes report using free time largely with their families (Pleck, 1975; Veroff, Douvan, & Kulka, 1981). Both sexes also report more general satisfaction with their families than from work (Campbell, Converse, & Rodgers, 1976). On all of these counts, the sexes do not differ significantly.

These findings do not contradict the fact that fathers spend less time with children than do mothers, nor deny that child care may mean different things to men than to women. The findings do suggest, however, that as individuals men may care about children more than commonly believed. Presumably, then, the process of developing professional commitments to children among men can be built on this base of positive personal feeling; the feeling need not be created in the first place. If early childhood educators have not built such commitment among very many men, then they may have failed for other reasons, some of which we will discuss.

FROM PERSONAL CONTRIBUTIONS
TO PROFESSIONAL COMMITMENTS

In early childhood education, male involvement with children has not kept pace with even the moderate levels found among fathers. The 100,000 practicing male teachers, of course, dedicate considerable effort to children; but male parents number in the millions, rather than in the thousands. Looked at another way, while male parents provide between one-sixth and one-third of all home child care, male teachers only provide about one-tenth of all early education. Evidently, parenting involves men with young children far more than does early childhood teaching.

From time to time, early childhood educators have advocated greater male involvement as professional teachers and child-care workers (Robinson, 1981). They have justified their support both for the sake of the children and for the sake of early childhood education as a profession. Ironically, some of these reasons are mutually contradictory, and this fact may explain why advocacy for male teachers has not led to dramatic changes in their numbers during the past two or three decades.

Compensation Hypotheses

Reasons focusing on the needs of the children might be called *compensation hypotheses*. These ideas all suggest that male teachers can somehow compensate for the lack of male involvement in some children's lives, especially in communities with large numbers of single, usually female, parents. In their strongest form, compensation hypotheses seem to assume—erroneously—that men are missing from most children's lives, rather than only from the lives of selected groups of children. In the most common version of this viewpoint, male teachers help young children's sex-role development. The help can occur in either of two ways: (1) by building boys' self-confidence and "sex-appropriate" behavior (Biller, 1974; Pleck, 1983), or (2) by offering children of both sexes a model of a caring, nurturant male (Seifert, 1975). Unfortunately, however, the two goals stem from conflicting values. The first implicitly favors traditional differences in gender roles, and the second implicitly opposes them. This conflict has either gone unnoticed by policy makers in early childhood education or has proved impossible to resolve, or perhaps a bit of both.

One problem with compensation hypotheses is that they expect particular embodiments of values from *all* male teachers and they assume particular needs within *all* young children. For their own good, young children are supposed to observe particular qualities in male teachers, whether these be the "old" manly ones or the "new" androgynous ones. In reality, however, children bring a variety of needs to school, and all teachers, male or female, are challenged to take these variations into account. In any one child-care center or class, not all children (or their parents) want androgyny, nor do they all want the same particular division of sex roles.

Social Equity Hypotheses

Reasons focusing on the needs of early childhood education as a profession might be called *social equity hypotheses* (Greenberg, 1985). Having more male teachers, according to this view, not only increases career options for men but also helps society to distinguish early childhood education from "women's work." This view takes no explicit position about the qualities of male teachers in the classroom or as professionals, nor about special male effects on children. Strictly speaking, therefore, it does not really contradict the compensation hypotheses.

In a democratic society, of course, social equity has a lot to recommend it. The most obvious beneficiaries would be men themselves: A visible male presence in early childhood education would probably stimulate still more men to consider this field more seriously as a career. In the long run, therefore, men would acquire a new career option, one that had previously been off limits psychologically and culturally. This change would be fair or equitable, providing that women in the meanwhile acquired new career options of their own. Otherwise, it could simply aggravate women's current disadvantages in the working world.

Less obvious, but still a beneficiary, would be the early childhood profession at large. According to social equity arguments, increasing the number of males working with young children would reduce the current tendency of early childhood educators to think of their job as "women's work," with all of the professional disadvantages connected with that image (Feiman-Nemser & Floden, 1986). Instead early childhood education teachers would more consistently think of their jobs as "professionals' work," and so, hopefully, would the public as well. Already, of course, many leaders in early childhood education think of themselves as professionals, but having larger numbers of men should strengthen this self-image and give the field more professional self-confidence.

Current stereotypes expect many things from early childhood teachers which are also expected of stereotypical mothers: passive compliance with the authorities, for one example, and lack of interest in personal and professional development, for another. These expectations are often not justified, but they can spoil teachers' pride in their work and make them wish they had chosen some other profession (Biklen, 1983; Feistritzer, 1983). In these ways, separating the notions of teaching and of womanhood might encourage professionalism in early childhood education.

But there are problems with social equity hypotheses, too. In society as a whole, beliefs in social equity must compete strongly with other cultural values, including beliefs in traditional gender roles. Therefore, not everyone can be expected to welcome larger numbers of males into early childhood education. It seems likely, for example, that some members of society (and even some existing female teachers) may feel that an influx of male teachers threatens female jobs. These reactions would resemble those that occur when women make their first appearance in previously all-male jobs (Schreiber, 1979).

Even if these fears do not constitute good reasons for keeping men out of early childhood education, they deserve consideration. What, in fact, would be the effects of larger numbers of men entering early childhood education? The answer to this question is necessarily speculative, but research on existing male teachers does suggest some preliminary ideas about it.

QUALITIES OF MALE TEACHERS OF YOUNG CHILDREN

So far, research on male teachers of young children has focused on three issues: their personal and professional backgrounds, their styles of classroom teaching, and their long-term attitudes about early childhood education as a career. According to current findings, men differ substantially from women only in the last of these three areas.

Personal and Professional Background

In spite of the potential usefulness of such information, little is known about the personal backgrounds of early childhood teachers, whether male or female. At present, the best guesses about their backgrounds must extend or extrapolate from surveys of related groups, such as elementary school teachers. The latter group, by all reports, come from relatively modest economic backgrounds, include more than their share of persons with low academic ability, and yet account for one of the largest proportions of university degrees of any profession (Feistritzer, 1983). As it happens, all of these features occur more strongly among male elementary teachers than among female ones (NEA, 1982). On the average, that is, men who teach elementary school come from more modest economic backgrounds than do women; include more low-ability persons as students-in-training; and yet account for more university degrees than do women.

Whether these sex differences also occur among early childhood teachers, however, is not certain. The small number of men in this field, in particular, poses a problem in drawing parallels with elementary teachers. As an extremely select group, the males stand more chance of differing somehow from other male teachers and of differing from female early childhood teachers as well. As a group, male early childhood teachers have contradicted many more gender expectations than usual. This fact suggests a need to learn what these individuals have experienced that allowed them to do so. Did they persevere, for example, or were they just oblivious to social prejudices? Male early childhood teachers, it seems, are unique enough to deserve their own demographic survey; they are numerous enough to lend themselves to it; and yet they are invisible enough not to have been surveyed yet.

Classroom Teaching Style

Under current circumstances, men who teach young children do not adopt teaching styles much different from those of women who teach young children (Lee & Wolinsky, 1973). Both sexes initiate activities at about the same frequency; both offer similar arrays of choices to children (art, stories, snack, and the like); both respond to disruptive behavior in similar ways. Existing gender differences stem more from differences in amounts of classroom experience that teachers have. The less experienced gender (males) behaves much like less experienced teachers in general; for example, men rely comparatively more on children's initiatives for selecting activities and engage in more rough-and-tumble play (Gold & Reis, 1982).

Because of a scarcity of highly experienced males, however, we do not know whether experienced male teachers would necessarily resemble experienced female teachers. Although it is tempting to think so, gender differences in personal and professional backgrounds might alter their long-run teaching styles; that is, with experience, males might eventually begin to diverge from females in this field. Studies of the socialization of other teachers support this hypothesis (Hoy & Rees, 1977; Sprinthall & Thies-Sprinthall, 1983). In elementary schools, in particular, beginners tend to be impressed by the work of veteran teachers and imitate their conduct as closely as possible. On the whole, elementary teachers do not report feeling in control of their own teaching style until many years into their classroom careers—longer than most males currently have worked in early childhood education.

Note also that, even if teaching behaviors look similar, they may not be perceived as similar if performed by members of different sexes. This possibility seems especially likely in situations that are strongly associated with just one gender, such as early childhood classrooms. A female teacher's noncommittal response to a child's anger, for example, may look like gentle patience to the uninitiated observer; but a similarly ambiguous response by a male teacher may look like an effort to restrain the teacher's own anger. Research about impression formation suggests that such reinterpretations occur widely; that is, particular attitudes, behaviors, and personal qualities take on very different meanings, depending on the sex of the person who shows them (Deaux & Lewis, 1984). If males adopt the normal, usual styles of early childhood teaching, therefore, at least some of their behavior may not seem "normal" or "usual" to some parents and children.

Long-term Orientation Toward Teaching

The lack of classroom style differences suggests that, if gender differences exist among early childhood teachers, they have to do with long-run orientation toward teaching. Research confirms this possibility for elementary school teachers: At this level of schooling, women remain in the classroom for more years than do men, either through choice or through lack of alternatives (Sadker & Sadker, 1985). Men, for their part, seek administrative work sooner and more frequently than do females. According to conventional wisdom, furthermore, men also become more frustrated than women with classroom work as the years go by. Some research has supported this idea (Lortie, 1975), but other research finds that both sexes become equally frustrated (Spencer, 1986).

During the first 5 to 10 years of early childhood teaching, however, men and women show rather similar attitudes about their work. Detailed interviews of male teachers of young children find some hints of frustrated ambition among them, but only hints (Seifert, 1984). Even after several years, both sexes appear to enjoy the classroom, express a desire to remain working in it, and also express a desire to leave it "eventually." When the men in Seifert's study did express interest in nonclassroom work, their alternatives usually concerned other services to children. Instead of teaching a kindergarten class, for example, a man would aspire to work in a city recreation program. Contrary to popular expectations, relatively few males aspired to become school administrators. These results essentially parallel those found among female teachers (Biklen, 1983), but they are more surprising to discover in males.

WHY DO MEN REMAIN A MINORITY?

In spite of their relatively strong involvement with children as parents, why have men remained such a small proportion of early childhood educators? Two reasons have already been suggested in this chapter. The first is the way that male teachers are justified to society: Sometimes the reasons conflict and therefore cause little net increase in support among parents and policy makers. The second reason has to do with the structure of early childhood teaching: This job seems to require more fixed units of commitment to children than does parenting. This fact may not be fair to women in society generally, who often also experience "fixed units of commitment" as mothers. But it may affect males as teachers more strongly than women as mothers, since men can probably find alternatives to early childhood teaching more easily than women can find alternatives to motherhood.

In addition, however, at least three other reasons exist for low male involvement. First, the very poor salaries and working conditions in early childhood education probably encourage men, more than women, to look elsewhere for employment. This happens partly because men are socialized to evaluate jobs more exclusively by their long-term career opportunities, and partly because society offers men more alternative forms of employment, most of which pay substantially more than working with young children. On the whole, women have fewer occupations to choose from and most of these are poorly paid. That many women nonetheless enjoy working with young children intensely probably shows the intrinsic viability of early childhood education as a profession, as much as female "indifference" to low pay.

Second, the gender biases that pervade society at large seem to affect early childhood educators as well. One survey found, for example, that preservice education students rate typical male education students as significantly less suitable for early childhood education, compared to their female peers (Seifert, 1983). Similar biases exist among experienced teachers as well. A recent study of educators in Oklahoma, for example, found that teachers of both sexes—but especially men—associated the teaching role with a variety of female virtues, such as intuitive sensitivity and lack of ambition (Patrick, Griswold, & Vaughn-Robertson, 1986). The teachers did not, however, associate these virtues nearly so strongly with women's role in general. In evaluating women's role, in fact, teachers approximated the relatively liberal attitudes of other professionals in Oklahoma, while in evaluating teachers' role they were significantly more gender-typed or traditional.

Third, the widely reported isolation of classroom teaching may help to maintain constant proportions of the genders among teachers, whatever that mix happens to be currently. Isolation achieves this result by its contradictory effects on individual teachers. On the one hand, isolation may make some teachers—male or female—feel unwanted and unrespected. Individual teachers probably will attribute these feelings to a variety of causes: to being inexperienced, for example, or to being female (for women) or being a minority (for men). On the other hand, the isolation of the classroom may also protect dedicated male teachers from the worst expressions of discrimination or disrespect. This protection may not help to recruit men into early childhood teaching in the first place, but it may help some men feel better (less hassled) about their choice once they are in. All things considered, the net result will be the status quo: protection for some males but demoralization for others, whether male or female. If male teachers therefore happen to form a minority, then isolation will tend to keep them a minority.

Note that explicit discrimination probably does not strongly affect male involvement in early childhood education. Interviews with experienced male kindergarten teachers suggest that discrimination does occur but also that such discrimination is only occasional (Seifert, 1984). Among the 20 men interviewed, for example, about half described incidents that they considered discriminatory. Principals refused to allow them to teach the youngest children in a particular school, for example, and male teachers encountered conflicts with their own mothers and fathers when they first entered early childhood teaching. But none of the men in Seifert's study considered such experiences major obstacles to their professional development, and half never mentioned any such incidents at all. If discriminatory incidents interfere with male involvement, therefore, they probably do so primarily among would-be male teachers, by making men expect that they will experience difficulties once they actually begin work.

THE FUTURE FOR MEN
IN EARLY CHILDHOOD EDUCATION

This chapter has proposed that men have much more involvement with young children as parents than as teachers. This fact suggests that there is potential for greater male involvement as early childhood teachers than in the past. Men, it seems, may be avoiding early childhood education not primarily because they dislike children, but for other reasons, such as poor pay and historical inertia. From these ideas follows the most crucial argument: Recruiting more men would enhance the professional self-image of early childhood education. But it would not necessarily compensate for any gender-role deficits or needs in the children we serve; arguing that it would, in fact, may actually be beside the point.

Research supports these ideas, at least for the immediate future. If additional males in early childhood education resemble those who currently work in this field, then recruiting more men will *not* change the background characteristics of the early childhood education teaching force very much. Nor will more men affect daily, typical classroom practices. More men will, however, bring stronger long-run commitments to sustained work, and they will help to distinguish the nurturing, caring, and teaching roles of early childhood education from their current stereotype as "women's work."

Over the longer term, though, recruiting more men may have other effects, which by their nature are currently hard to anticipate. Very large numbers of men, for example, would probably lead to new sorts of individuals—both male and female—entering early childhood education. At present, though, the personalities and backgrounds of these people can only be guessed at. Presumably they would continue to have the strong dedication to children's learning and development that current early childhood educators so often show. But they might also enter early childhood education with a strong expectation of joining a true profession, one that no longer operates in near poverty level conditions, and in which colleagues are both able and willing to share ideas and time with each other.

REFERENCES

Biklen, S. (1983). *Teaching as an occupation for women.* Syracuse, NY: Education Designs Group.
Biller, H. (1974). *Paternal deprivation: Family, school, sexuality and society.* Lexington, MA: Heath.

Campbell, A., Converse, P., & Rodgers, W. (1976). *The quality of American life*. New York: Russell Sage.

Deaux, K., & Lewis, L. (1984). Structure of gender stereotypes: Interrelationships among components and gender labels. *Journal of Personality and Social Psychology, 46*, 991–1004.

Feiman-Nemser, S., & Floden, R. (1986). The cultures of teaching. In M. Wittrock (Ed.), *Handbook of research on teaching* (3rd ed.) (pp. 505–526). New York: Macmillan.

Feistritzer, E. (1983). *The American teacher*. Washington, DC: Feistritzer Publications.

Greenberg, S. (1985). Educational equity in early education environments. In S. Klein (Ed.), *Handbook for achieving sex equity through education* (pp. 457–469). Baltimore, MD: Johns Hopkins University Press.

Gold, D., & Reis, M. (1982). Male teacher effects on young children. *Sex Roles, 8*, 492–513.

Hoffman, L. (1984). Work, family, and the socialization of the child. In R. Parke (Ed.), *Review of child development research: Vol. 7, The family* (pp. 223–282). Chicago: University of Chicago Press.

Hoy, W., & Rees, R. (1977). The bureaucratic socialization of student teachers. *Journal of Teacher Education, 28*, 23–26.

Kimmel, M. (Ed.). (1987). *Changing men: New directions in research on men and masculinity*. Beverly Hills, CA: Sage.

Lee, P., & Wolinsky, A. (1973). Male teachers of young children. *Young Children, 28*, 342–352.

Lortie, D. (1975). *Schoolteacher*. Chicago: University of Chicago Press.

National Association for the Education of Young Children. (1985). *In Whose Hands?* (Report #760). Washington, DC: Author.

National Education Association. (1982). *The status of the American public school teacher*. Washington, DC: Author.

Patrick, A., Griswold, R., & Vaughn-Robertson, A. (1986). Domestic ideology and the teaching profession. *Issues in Education, 3*, 139–157.

Pleck, J. (1979). The theory of male sex role identity: Its rise and fall, 1936 to the present. In M. Lewin (Ed.), *In the shadow of the past: Psychology portrays the sexes*. New York: Columbia University Press.

Pleck, J. (1983). Husbands' paid work and family roles. In L. Lopata (Ed.), *Research on the interweave of social roles: Jobs and families* (Vol. 3) (pp. 251–333). Greenwich, CT: JAI Press.

Pleck, J. (1985). *Working wives/working husbands*. Beverly Hills, CA; Sage.

Robinson, B. (1981). Changing views on male early childhood teachers. *Young Children, 36*, 27–48.

Sadker, D., & Sadker, M. (1985). The treatment of sex equity in teacher education. In S. Klein (Ed.), *Handbook for achieving sex equity through education*. Baltimore, MD: Johns Hopkins University Press.

Schreiber, C. (1979). *Changing places: Men and women in transitional occupations*. Cambridge, MA: MIT Press.

Seifert, K. (1975). The best men for child care work. *Child Welfare, 4*, 188–193.

Seifert, K. (1983, April). *Suitability and competence of men who teach young children*. Paper presented at the annual meeting of the American Educational Research Association, Montreal, Canada.

Seifert, K. (1984). Career experiences of men who teach young children. *Canadian Journal of Research on Early Childhood Education, 1,* 55–67.

Spencer, D. A. (1986). *Contemporary women teachers: Balancing home and school.* New York: Longmans.

Sprinthall, N., & Thies-Sprinthall, L. (1983). The teacher as an adult learner: A cognitive-developmental approach. In G. Griffin (Ed.), *Staff development: 82nd Yearbook of the National Society for Studies in Education.* Chicago: University of Chicago Press.

U.S. Bureau of the Census. (1985). *Statistical abstract of the United States.* Washington, DC: U.S. Government Printing Office.

Veroff, J., Douvan, E., & Kulka, R. (1981). *The inner American.* New York: Basic Books.

10 • On Becoming Knowledgeable Professionals

JONATHAN G. SILIN
Long Island Association for AIDS Care

The professionalization agenda of early childhood educators, including the emphasis on credentials, licensing, nomenclature, and public relations, is geared toward standardizing practices and improving the status of the field. This agenda was set in motion years before national attention focused on the quality of teaching at all levels of schooling. Better salaries, improved working conditions, and increased educational responsibility, the hoped-for outcomes of professionalization, are clearly warranted and appropriate goals for which to strive. However, the strategy for attaining these ends, namely, the professionalization of workers and their field of work, is more problematic than is generally assumed. It is the purpose of this chapter to explore some of the potential meanings of professionalism as it is currently being advocated within the field of early education.

In the past, critical sociologists have examined the meaning of professionalism from a variety of perspectives. Larson (1977), for example, details how the professions in general act as a conserving force in society, supporting the status quo and reinforcing class divisions. Grace (1978) explores the ways in which appeals to professionalism may serve as a form of social control which prevents teachers from understanding education as a political process and themselves as political agents. Professionalism may thus alienate teachers from the real meaning of their work. Apple (1983) further suggests that claims to professionalism obscure the deskilling and proletarianization of teaching in postindustrial countries, thereby masking the actual loss of autonomy experienced by most teachers today. Ozga and Lawn (1981) take a more balanced view, maintaining that, while the ideology of professionalism may be used by those in power to divert teachers from seeing their true interests as members of the working class by falsely encouraging them to identify with employers rather than with other workers, it may also be used by teachers themselves to assert their right to self-determination and control of their craft. Some theorists have suggested that teachers and salaried white-collar workers constitute a new aspect of the petty bourgeoisie (Poulantzas, 1973), an ambiguously located segment of the labor force (Wright, 1976), or part of the working class (Ozga & Lawn, 1981). How teachers identify themselves affects the way they relate to various groups of students, their employers, and social change movements (Grace, 1978).

THE EARLY CHILDHOOD KNOWLEDGE BASE

One of the often-mentioned but seldom-articulated themes in the literature of professionalism, the knowledge base that grounds claims to professional status, seems to have special relevance to early childhood education. Historically, professions have sought to establish a monopoly over the provision of a particular service through the negotiation of cognitive exclusiveness, that is, the possession of a unique body of information and skills. For public service professionals such as teachers and social workers, this is especially significant, since their claims to authority cannot as easily be based on organizational position as can those of technobureaucrats (i.e., school superintendents), or on traditional ideals as can those of independent "market" professionals (i.e., lawyers and physicians).

Early childhood educators (Spodek & Saracho, 1982) have expressed concern about the lack of a highly developed body of knowledge and a reduced emphasis on theoretical and conceptual work within the field. Some (Ade, 1982; Joffe, 1977) have pleaded for the creation and/or systematization of a unique fund of knowledge so that professional status might be assured. But what can be said of the body of knowledge that early childhood educators currently claim as their own? Where does it come from, and how does it function for practitioners? In what ways might it support or impede the current press for professional status?

There are significant distinctions between the field of child psychology and child development, as well as between the work of clinical and experimental psychologists. However, most psychologists focus on the growth and learning style of the child rather than on the values and purposes of the adult, the ethical commitments of educators, or on the politics and social structures of the community—the objective context in which education occurs.

While the 19th-century kindergarten movement in America was catalyzed by the religiously inspired work of Froebel, the 20th-century field of early education has been most strongly influenced by various kinds of psychologists. Even as the early progressives focused attention on the direct observation of children and the use of their daily interests as the locus of curriculum, the informally structured child-study movement began to lose ground to the more rigorous science of child development. By the 1920s, behaviorist theories of learning and the measurement movement, as well as a concern for the formation of proper habits, dominated the field. During the 1930s, the nursery school was more affected by Freudian theory. In the 1940s and 1950s, the normative studies of children done by Gesell at Yale firmly took hold, signaling wide acceptance of the child development point of view (Jersild, 1946).

The psychologistic orientation of educators became even more pronounced in the 1960s with the proliferation of Head Start models. Psychological criteria, whether affective, cognitive, or social, became the basis for educational decision making; psychology became education's primary "supply" discipline. Thus, theoretical discussions about curricular goals were predicated upon distinctions within psychological rather than educational paradigms (Kohlberg & Mayer, 1972). Training programs for new teachers proposed to reflect different approaches to development (Seaver & Cartwright, 1977), teacher praxis was analyzed in terms of the psychological theory employed by the practitioner (Porter, 1981), and programatic innovations were evaluated in terms of developmental appropriateness (Elkind, 1981).

The discourse of early childhood education continues to give precedence to psychological considerations, acknowledging offhandedly that other concerns may be of importance (Silin, 1986). But these concerns, often referred to as philosophical or value related and rarely as economically or politically relevant, seldom receive full treatment in the literature of the field. For example, Evans (1982), in his description of the components of early childhood programs, states that their theoretical foundations rest equally in philosophical and psychological thought. But when he refers to the terms currently used to identify different models—behaviorist, dynamic, constructivist—he unwittingly reveals the dominance of the latter over the former.

Perhaps the often-commented-upon tension and lack of communication between practitioner and researcher (e.g., Katz, 1977) can in part be attributed to this belief that knowledge about early education settings should be created by developmentalists rather than educators themselves. Because educators are the lower-status group, supposedly concerned with practice rather than theory, it has been too easily assumed that their interests might be subsumed under the interests of the more prestigious group. But those who choose to see early childhood education as a unique cultural system with its own history, tradition, and values suggest otherwise (Takanishi, 1981). They point out that, because early educators go through a specific socialization process, they see children and development differently from child development specialists. And because they work in classrooms rather than universities, they have a different perspective on understanding early education settings.

Nevertheless, the literature of child development and growth remains the primary base for educational decisions about young children in school. As Bettye Caldwell (1984), past president of NAEYC, confidently summarized, "Our field represents the applied side of the basic science of child development" (p. 53). But if early educators only apply the knowledge gained by others, how can it be said that they possess, or might create, a unique grounding for their work? Is it therefore even possible for early childhood education to meet one of the traditional criteria for professionalization—cognitive exclusiveness? More important, how might a limited developmental perspective work against the broader educational purposes of practitioners in classrooms?

Spodek (1970) has questioned the role of psychology in education, making an important distinction between curriculum sources, as "a set of goals which are the aims of education" (p. 6), and resources that are the means for achieving these ends. Fein and Schwartz (1982) also make a distinction between theories of development and theories of practice. Although they note that the activist nature of theories of practice involves the choice of behaviors that the educator desires to nurture, the primary thrust of their argument demonstrates that a theory of practice is little more than an elaborated theory of development. Articulating the differences between the two types of theory, using the work of Bowlby, Berlyne, and Piaget, they perpetuate the notion that educational practice begins with developmental knowledge. Egan (1983) has asserted that the specific function of educational theory, as opposed to psychological theory, is to tell us how to design curricula to produce educated people; hence, there is a concern for the kind of person who will result from the educational process. A theory of education is not only a theory of individual growth but also a theory of political and social power. If the goal of education is to inculcate the knowledge and skills that will prepare persons to be successful political and social agents, then it must be informed by a sense of the *polis* that the student will eventually enter.

From this perspective, psychological theory must be part of a more inclusive theory of education. The former becomes meaningful in the context of the latter. The role of education is to shape the forces that produce psychological regularities, not to be bound by them. This situation is the case because psychological research focuses on behaviors and thoughts that are the result of personal and historical experience. Psychology reflects what has been and what is, but not necessarily what ought to be. Psychologists may also isolate particular skills or characteristics for study, with the goal of increasing knowledge rather than effecting change in a given situation. The growing critique of Piaget's work illustrates the hidden biases of much psychological research (Silin, 1987).

In contrast, the work of educators is more clearly culture bound and value saturated because it prepares children to live within specific communities and traditions. It must be concerned not only with cognitive and socioemotional skills but also with erudition and learning. Educated people need to be able to think clearly and to make wise choices as to what they will think about.

Given the saliency of political theory and ethical commitment to educational practice, it is appropriate to ask why they have been minimalized in early childhood discourse. Why have we been more open to knowledge about development than to analysis of the context in which we live and the valuing processes that inform our work?

"SAFE" KNOWLEDGE AND PROFESSIONAL IDENTITY

A concern for bettering the circumstances of the poor was one of the distinguishing characteristics of those who first created early education programs; this theme connects the work of such diverse individuals as Rachel and Margaret Macmillan, Marie Montessori, Robert Owen, and Johann Pestalozzi. The location of kindergartens in settlement houses and the structuring of teachers' days so that they might make home visits in the afternoon was part of this commitment. As was the case with later progressive reformers, educational strategies for young children were integrated into broad social visions (Almy, 1975).

It is true that, for a brief period during the War on Poverty, early educators tried to address the issue of the relationship of social class, curriculum, and schooling outcomes. This interest took the form of a debate over the nature of compensatory education. While some (Bereiter & Engelmann, 1966) argued that children of the poor needed more academically oriented programs in order to catch up to their middle-class peers, others (Biber, Shapiro, & Wickens, 1971) maintained that all children, regardless of background, benefited from the same kind of developmentally oriented approach. From the beginning of this debate, a few (Lazerson, 1971) were skeptical of the ability of educators to effect changes that were more properly required in the economic system outside the classroom. The majority of educators, however, seemed to have been caught up in the belief that education could in fact equalize opportunity and create a more just society. This early enthusiasm has since tempered, and interest in compensatory education has been subsumed under discussions of the value of bilingual and multicultural programs, thus masking economic issues.

The limited response of early childhood educators to the serious critique of American education begun in the 1960s may be explained in part by the weaknesses of the critiques themselves, their failure to address early education, and the disturbing nature of their analyses insofar as they did pertain to progressive methods. This critical literature begins with the work of revisionist historians (Katz, 1971; Tyack, 1974) who described the failure of the schools to promote social mobility, equality of opportunity, and democratic forms of interaction. It includes the radical critics (Illich, 1970; Kohl, 1967) who focused on issues of depersonalization, apathy, and alienation; and the educationists (Giroux, 1980; Macdonald, 1975) who analyzed the nature of curricula, overt and covert, and the way that they were structured to fulfill the needs of the postindustrial workplace. It also should be noted that the work of critical sociologists (Bernstein, 1975; Sharp & Green, 1978) on the British infant schools had special implications for early education. Although their general conclusion that open, progressive methods offer increased opportunity for social control was foreshadowed in Gramsci's (1971) writings, it was new to many American readers.

Another reason for limited response to these critiques is that practitioners prefer to see themselves as subjective and apolitical, concerned only with the best interests of the child. Silin (1982) found early educators to understand their work in terms of protective control; that is, they viewed children as open to the world, curious and eager to learn, yet vulnerable to the threats posed by either internal emotional turmoil or external sources of influence. Thus they saw their task as one of protecting children through controlling the educational environment.

An emphasis on developmentally adequate curricula allowed teachers to think that they were noncoercive, unprejudiced practitioners. Because children were viewed as vulnerable and fragile, teachers did not want to see themselves as influencing them in any way that had ideological or political ramifications. Their job was to facilitate, to enable children to learn and grow. They did not seem to recognize the degree to which different developmental schema speak to different aspects of growth and embody particular values and diverse conceptions of human possibility. Nor did they seem to possess a sense of choice about their work, which would indicate that they saw themselves as self-determining agents rather than as beneficent technicians responding to the demands of their charges.

This self-image of early childhood teachers reflects the progressive belief that it is possible to "keep politics out of the school" and the traditional American belief that schools function in an objective manner so as to allow the talented to succeed on merit alone. Perhaps, too, it reflects the gender of the early educators and the social expectations of their role. From the first, this role was modeled on images of maternal nurture, and it is indeed difficult to think of maternal nurture in terms of political practice or social empowerment. In the early 19th century, women were encouraged to enter teaching, at least until their own child-bearing years. It was argued that their instincts allowed them to know children better and to manage them with ease:

> That females are incomparably better teachers for young children than males, can not admit of doubt. Their manner is more mild and gentle, and hence more in consonance with the tenderness of childhood. They are endowed by nature with the stronger parental impulses, and this makes the society of children delightful, and turns duty into pleasure. . . . They are also of purer morals. [Elsbree, 1939, p. 201]

While early childhood theoreticians such as Pestalozzi (1907) also idealized the mother as the first teacher, and others such as Montessori (1966) spoke of early education as "communizing a maternal function" (p. 66), it is clear that for most the common ground shared by child and adult was a devalued ground, ruled by emotionality and impulse. Women teachers were able to develop the character and moral behaviors so valued by such school reformers in America as Horace Mann and Henry Barnard, but later intellectual achievements were to be guided by men:

> In childhood the intellectual faculties are but partially developed—the affection much more fully. At that early age the affections are the key to the whole thing. The female teacher readily possesses herself of that key, and thus having access to the heart, the mind is soon reached and operated upon. [Elsbree, 1939, p. 203]

The low status and pay offered to women does not negate the significance that teaching had for them, nor does it suggest the pride, enthusiasm, and professionalism with which many approached their work (Hoffman, 1980). For working-class and lower-middle-class women who went into the public schools, teaching was the only way to achieve a modicum of respectable independence. For upper-middle-class women who gravitated toward the early childhood movement, teaching was a means for realizing their interests in social reform (Snyder, 1972). The commitment was to the child's growth and development and to the context in which it occurred.

TECHNOCRATIC-MINDEDNESS IN EDUCATION

Finally, as members of a field without social or economic recognition, early childhood educators have sought professional status through asserting the scientific knowledge base (i.e., child development theory) of their practice. Professionalization has always involved claims to a specialized body of knowledge and specific set of skills that permit the performance of a unique service. But it has been argued that the important decisions in the educational sphere are not technical or scientific but moral, based on differing conceptions of the good, the true, and the beautiful (Spodek, 1977). Thus the drive for professionalism contributes to an undue scientism within the early childhood enterprise. Ethical, moral, or aesthetic languages, which more fully address the educational domain, are not highly prized in our culture, which celebrates technical empirical knowledge.

Many educational researchers reflect such a technocratic-mindedness in their work. For example, Lortie (1975) was disappointed because an analysis of his interviews with teachers showed "a low proportion of words which are not commonly used; since the interview dealt with teaching, it should have elicited a technical vocabulary" (p. 73). Jackson (1968) further criticizes teachers for their "tendency to rely on spontaneous expressions of interest and enthusiasm of their students rather than on scientific or objective measures" and for their "conceptual simplicity" (p. 144). Dreeben (1970) calls for the development of a more highly defined "technology" of teaching as the only means of increasing the level of professionalism.

This technocratic-mindedness is a mode of thought that has come to dominate many aspects of thinking and acting in the postindustrial world (Bowers, 1982). Presuming to define both legitimate ways of knowing and legitimate sources of knowledge, the technical perspective has two primary components. The first is the belief that all problems are scientific and technological in nature and can be solved through the application of positivist, scientific principles. The second is the assertion that science itself can provide an adequate knowledge base for describing and defining all human experience. Assuming a radical distinction between fact and value, object and subject, knowledge and knower, the technical perspective devalues nonscientific forms of knowing—symbolic/interpretive, intuitive/precognitive, critical/reflective, and aesthetic. Because it gives precedence to the abstract, theoretical, and logical over the concrete, particular, and prelogical, it also negates the lived reality of historical and cultural contexts (Broughton & Zahaykevich, 1982).

The reliance on child development research as a knowledge base for educational practice is a potent form of technocratic-mindedness. It takes decision making out of the realm of moral and political consideration to which it more properly belongs. The developmental, "individual-needs" language of early educators masks the function of their work. Different approaches to development reflect alternative values and world views. It is this realization that can require practitioners to accept a broader interpretation of their function and the knowledge base in which it is grounded. Age-related differences should not be obscured in the creation of educational environments; nevertheless, what age means needs to be explored from many perspectives, including the psychological. Knowledge about how people change over time must be part of an articulated social philosophy if it is to be used effectively.

KNOWLEDGEABLE PROFESSIONALS

My objective has been to suggest how one aspect of the professionalism project—the claim to a discrete, scientific knowledge base—reinforces a technocratic-mindedness that ultimately subverts teachers from achieving real power by denying them the right to define their own knowledge and by denying them access to other forms of knowledge appropriate to understanding educational practice.

Revitalizing the Knowledge Base

The knowledge base of the field of early childhood education clearly bears reconsideration. Three aspects of a renewed knowledge base, consistent with the historical features that have given shape to the early childhood field, present themselves for consideration.

Balance of disciplines. First, early education must become permeable to influences from many disciplines in addition to psychology. For example, greater attention to knowledge of sociology and history can serve to balance the often abstracted and decontextualized way that mainstream psychology looks at children. Without such a perspective, an unrealistic emphasis on individual development may dominate the field, to the neglect of the social realities of everyday life. In one of the few attempts to assess the economic implications of the expansion of early education, Chamboredon and Prevort (1975) stress the need for a change in our thinking:

> The conditions for understanding nursery-school exercises flow from the conditions for inventing these exercises. . . . The proper objective of a sociology of nursery-school practice is the analysis of the lag between the functions delegated to the school by different social classes and the functions which it objectively tends to fulfill. [p. 334]

The concern is not only with alleviating the social ills created by poverty, as suggested by the first early childhood educators, but also with looking at how educational institutions themselves help to reproduce or promote resistance to underlying socioeconomic structures.

Schooling, even nursery schooling, is one of the central ways that society organizes power and influence. Recognizing this means that early education should not be exempt from a more political analysis of its program. Educators themselves need to delineate the political theory that inevitably lies behind all programs. Teaching needs to be viewed as more than the professionalization of a maternal function that occurs in a protective environment. It must be seen in the context of the larger societal processes that both shape and are shaped by it. Even the smallest pedagogical acts may have meaning for students that extends beyond the classroom. If teachers are to be more fully in control of their professional lives, they must assess this meaning and incorporate it into their knowledge base.

Historical and political analyses alone are not enough, for they refer to the past and the present but not necessarily to the future. A grounding in philosophy would encourage educators to think about the kinds of people they want to see emerging from the educational process and the nature of the society they want to build. It would also enable them to evaluate programs and trends as they appear. With more and more prepackaged and prestructured materials on the market, teachers need to be able to ask whether their use is consistent with their values and goals for children.

Exploration of alternative modes of knowing. While a better grasp of the traditional disciplines may help educators to understand the social implications of their work, an expanded knowledge base also includes investigation of alternative modes of knowing. This will affect both how children are viewed and curriculum implemented. The use of universal, theoretical constructs can obfuscate the complex realities of children's lives. Some within the field have already adopted a phenomenological approach to children, emphasizing the uniqueness and integrity of each child. As defined by Weber (1984), this means that "the existential moment-by-moment environmental interaction of the learner supersedes an interest in—even a recognition of—developmental factors. The departure from stage theory is in part out of discomfiture with a designated end point for all children" (p. 206).

Literature and the arts can also provide access to knowing children and childhood. Novels, plays, and films can frequently stimulate new insights into children's realities as well as our own. Imaginative constructions of fictional events can be as evocative and helpful as scientific descriptions of developmental processes. While it was once important to emphasize the uniqueness of young children as a group in order to draw attention to their special needs, perhaps it is now time to look at the continuities as well as the differences between children and adults. Such investigations of the commonalities between the generations, often hidden in hierarchically organized stage theories of development, find their roots in the writings of 19th-century Romantics like Coleridge, who proudly proclaimed that "to carry on the feeling of childhood into the powers of manhood . . . is the character and privilege of genius" (Walsh, 1959, p. 18). To acknowledge that children possess a moral integrity, a power of vision that has become submerged in adults, is to acknowledge that education itself is a form of moral persuasion, embodying values, promoting ways of being, and teaching ethical behaviors that are less subject to the laws of empirical validation than to the rigors of democratic discourse and the problems of intersubjective communication.

As early educators incorporate a variety of knowledge sources into their own understanding of children, they might give renewed emphasis in the curriculum itself to multiple modalities for experiencing the world. Teachers of young children have long accepted an artistic-aesthetic component in the curriculum as a way of promoting personal expression. But this aspect of curriculum also has a perceptual/cognitive aspect. This is not to say that aesthetics are a tool for cognitive instruction but rather that they provoke self-reflection and understanding. The aesthetic can help children to break with the taken-for-granted world and open new possibilities, creating privileged moments when new visions are achieved (Greene, 1978).

Similarly, while early educators have always paid attention to physical development and growth, recent thinking has suggested the centrality of the body as a vehicle for learning. Linking language, thought, and sensuous experience of the self in the world, Levin (1982) describes a new grounding for teaching moral valuing, while Grumet (1985), drawing on diverse philosophical sources, asks us to rethink the meaning and learning of reading.

Many curricularists today are writing in response to the growing technocratic-mindedness that fosters educational environments in which control, certainty, and quantification are given precedence over imagination, wonder, and intuition. Promoting an appreciation of the mythic, poetic, and cultural is not to foster the irrational but to expand the definition of rational beyond the technical. A rich, multilayered education of the imagination can supersede a narrow, unidimensional education of technical competence.

Creation of a research base.   Finally, early childhood specialists need to create their own research base (Caldwell, 1984). Inadequate descriptions of the teaching role, imposition of inappropriate theoretical constructs, and impractical or incomplete curriculum recommendations have too often resulted from the distance between practitioners and researchers from outside the field (Almy, 1982). This growing dichotomy between those who produce knowledge and those who use it appears to be an inevitable outcome of the positivist methodologies and technocratic-mindedness that pervade education today (Fay, 1975).

Especially relevant to a revitalized knowledge base in early childhood is the incorporation of the new scholarship on women in education. This scholarship underlines the need to reconceptualize our ideas of what research is and who does it. Historical researches conducted by men tend to record women's experience, if at all, as incidental and inessential (Tetreault & Schmuck, 1985). In most histories men are the subject and women are the other, differentiated only in terms of the male experience. Shakeshaft (1986) has explored the facts that shaped women's professional lives as researchers, noting their marginality and isolation from the mainstream, which largely ignored their work. Techniques for uncovering the history of early education must move beyond traditional methods, to identify contributors who may not have been part of a university community or other male-dominated organization. Our definition of the nature of research—work that formed the basis of programs but did not receive academic acknowledgment—will need expansion, as will the sources we explore. Diaries, letters, and school reports will have to be added to traditional treatises on educational practice and philosophy.

In addition, it has been suggested that there is a basic conflict between researchers, who are theoretically oriented, and practitioners, who are more clinically focused (Sergiovanni, 1985). Teachers aim at action, not knowledge per se. They are "truth makers," constructing social worlds, rather than "truth seekers," looking for the right solution to a problem. Teachers tend to emphasize indeterminacy and uncertainty rather than regularity and scientific law. They rely heavily on their own experience and the experience of others in similar settings. Ultimately too, teachers need to believe in what they are doing, because they do not often see immediate results from their work. They cannot afford the detachment and healthy skepticism demanded of pure scientists.

Early childhood education needs a research literature that looks directly to child-care workers to define questions for investigation, to corroborate findings, and to insure practical meaning. This research would articulate the knowledge that already exists and make it accessible to others. It would give recognition to the unique perspectives of the early childhood educator. In recent years researchers have become more open to qualitative techniques involving ethnographic standards, interpretive interviews, and participant observations. They have increasingly come to understand the value of the teacher's personal practical knowledge and collaborative research strategies (Elbaz, 1983). Involving teachers in critical inquiry is to assume that they are capable of comprehending the complexity of schooling and of engaging in reflective action, an assumption that is not usually made in traditional, hierarchically structured modes of inquiry. True collaboration requires equal responsibility and status for both teacher and researcher, which is often hard to achieve in a real-world context that stresses competition, individual autonomy, and well-defined lines of authority (Oakes, Hare, & Sirotnik, 1986). Research employing good qualitative methods respects the intricacies of the teaching/learning situation, see the teacher as a whole person, and acknowledges his or her purposes and knowledge, consistently with the best traditions of the field.

The Language of Professionalism

Along with a renewed knowledge base, early childhood educators should come to recognize that the language of professionalism may have different meanings depending on the particular interest group using its terminology and the specific historical moment. Even within educational organizations, the rhetoric of professionalism has been frequently manipulated to maintain the dominance of a male power structure and to obscure the differences in interests between teachers and administrators.

In the 1920s and 1930s, the ideology of a united profession, supported by a belief in meritocratic and universalistic advancement, served to insure top-down management by males and to keep women out of decision-making positions (Tyack & Hansot, 1982). It was assumed that men had power because they were more committed and competent. Although many women once accepted second-class citizenship and internalized the male perspective on their capabilities, this is clearly changing. A recent study indicates that, while a good number of female teachers have not worked continuously or full time, which are traditional criteria for professional involvement, they always view themselves as career professionals (Biklen, 1985). Another study points out the gender bias of recent reports on education and their descriptions of professional leadership in the field (Tetreault & Schmuck, 1985).

As more women enter the workplace and assert their right to self-determination, standards of professionalism modeled on the male experience, as well as assumptions about the nature of professional commitment, will need to be reevaluated to reflect alternative career structures and interpretations of the meaning of work. This process has already begun in the writings of women who are seeking new representations of the teaching experience (Grumet, 1986; Pagano, 1985) and of men who have explored gender-related issues in contemporary educational contexts (Apple, 1983; Pinar, 1983).

Historically, the ideal projected by doctors and lawyers, the first professionals in preindustrial Europe, involved responsibility, client orientation, and ethical behavior. Professionals served the community and worked for the good of society. They were motivated by the value of work as an end in itself, rather than by entrepreneurial designs, and they were committed to a *noblesse oblige* ideal reflected in formal codes of ethics. In contemporary, postindustrial societies, it is the duty and service aspects of professionalism that have been stressed. Professionalism has all too often become a form of occupational control exercised by the state/employer over organizationally based employees. Professionals, in these contexts, should be concerned with standards within their fields of endeavor, act in a consultative rather than adversarial or advocacy role when dealing with those in power, and, above all, model responsible behavior by fostering a belief in the harmony of interests among potentially conflicting groups.

Needless to say, such a benign ideal belies the reality of how professional ideologies function, both inside and outside of the field. Authors such as Sarason (1982) make clear how the proliferation of professional identities within the school system after World War II intensified struggles over who had the right to deliver particular services and how these services would be perceived by others. Conflicts increased among professionals and between professional groups and administrators over decision-making powers. The banner of professionalism also affected the relationship of school staff to the clients they served. Because conflict was viewed as counterproductive, many did not see the potential for renewal contained in public pressure for change during the 1960s. The concern with professional status prevented educators from hearing or responding openly to demands that they share policy-making power. Respect for pluralism and democratic process was overshadowed by belief in expert knowledge and rationalized control of administrative hierarchies (Tyack & Hansot, 1982).

As the work of teaching becomes increasingly proletarianized through routinization, deskilling, and fragmentation; as teachers' salaries and working conditions continue to decline, it becomes imperative that the multiple meanings of professionalism be exposed. A review of recent proposals on the reform of teacher education suggests the contradictions of reports that proclaim the need to professionalize teaching yet make specific recommendations that leave teachers with little to do but implement standardized curricula created by experts (Cornbleth, 1986). Teacher workloads are frequently increased by curricular innovations that stress managerial efficiency and test scores, isolating teachers from professional peers and opportunities for substantive dialogue. The professional ideal of informed action based on reflective judgment becomes lost in the press to live up to externally imposed norms of productivity (Bullough & Gitlin, 1985).

Professionalism can be used to promote docility and occupational control by those in power. It can also be used as an occupational strategy by teachers, along with unionization, for resisting external control of the workplace and strengthening their positions relative to their employers. Here they draw on traditions of professionalism involving autonomy, expertise, and cognitive exclusiveness. The public service perspective of professionalism, although it discourages challenges to received opinion, may also be employed, since its inherent concern for others represents ideals that reach beyond the narrow interests of specific groups. In order to use professionalism as an effective occupational strategy, teachers must learn to reject the technocratic-mindedness embedded in traditional approaches to professionalism and professional knowledge and to see their interests as allied with those of other workers caught in the exigencies of the modern world.

REFERENCES

Ade, W. (1982). Professionalism and its implications for the field of early childhood education. *Young Children, 37*(3), 25–32.

Almy, M. (1975). *The early childhood educator at work.* New York: McGraw-Hill.

Almy, M. (1982, November). *An early childhood education/care research agenda.* Paper presented at the annual conference of the National Association for the Education of Young Children, Washington, DC.

Apple, M. (1983). Work, gender and teaching. *Teachers College Record, 84,* 611–629.

Bereiter, C., & Engelmann, S. (1966). *Teaching disadvantaged children in the preschool.* Englewood Cliffs, NJ: Prentice-Hall.

Bernstein, B. (1975). *Class, codes and control* (Vol. 3). London: Routledge & Kegan Paul.

Biber, B., Shapiro, E., & Wickens, D. (1971). *Promoting cognitive growth: A developmental-interaction point of view.* Washington, DC: National Association for the Education of Young Children.

Biklen, S. (1985). Can elementary school teaching be a career? A search for new ways of understanding women's work. *Issues in Education, 3,* 215–232.

Bowers, C. (1982). Locating the ideological foundations of a radical pedagogy. *Teachers College Record, 83,* 529–559.

Broughton, J., & Zahaykevich, M. (1982). The peace movement threat. *Teachers College Record, 84,* 152–173.

Bullough, R., & Gitlin, A. (1985). Schooling and change: A view from the lower rung. *Teachers College Record, 87,* 219–239.

Caldwell, B. (1984). Growth and development. *Young Children, 39*(6), 53–56.

Chamboredon, J. C., & Prevort, J. (1975). Changes in the social definition of early childhood. *Theory and Society, 3,* 331–350.

Cornbleth, C. (1986). Ritual and rationality in teacher education reform. *Educational Researcher, 15*(4), 5–15.

Dreeben, R. (1970). *The nature of teaching.* Glenview, IL: Scott, Foresman.

Egan, K. (1983). *Education and psychology.* New York: Teachers College Press.

Elbaz, F. (1983). *Teacher thinking: A study of practical knowledge.* New York: Nichols Publishing.

Elkind, D. (1981). *Children and adolescents.* New York: Oxford University Press.

Elsbree, W. (1939). *The American teacher: Evolution of a profession in a democracy.* New York: The American Book Company.

Evans, E. (1982). Curriculum models and early childhood education. In B. Spodek (Ed.), *Handbook of research in early childhood education* (pp. 107–134). New York: The Free Press.

Fay, B. (1975). *Social theory and political practice.* New York: Holmes & Meier.

Fein, G., & Schwartz, P. (1982). Developmental theories in early education. In B. Spodek (Ed.), *Handbook of research in early childhood education.* New York: Free Press.

Giroux, H. (1980). Critical theory and rationality in citizenship education. *Curriculum Inquiry, 10,* 329–367.

Grace, G. (1978). *Teachers, ideology and control.* London: Routledge & Kegan Paul.

Gramsci, A. (1971). *Selections from the prison notebooks* (Q. Hoare & G. Nowell-Smith, Eds.). London: Lawrence & Wishart.

Greene, M. (1978). *Landscapes of learning.* New York: Teachers College Press.

Grumet, M. (1985). Bodyreading. *Teachers College Record, 87,* 175–195.

Grumet, M. (1986, October). *The empty house: Furnishing education with feminist theory.* Paper presented at the Bergamo Conference on Curriculum Theory and Classroom Practice, Dayton, OH.

Hoffman, N. (1981). *Woman's "true" profession.* Old Westbury, NY: The Feminist Press.

Illich, I. (1970). *Deschooling society.* New York: Harper & Row.

Jackson, P. (1968). *Life in classrooms.* New York: Holt.

Jersild, A. (1946). *Child development and the curriculum.* New York: Bureau of Publication, Teachers College, Columbia University.

Joffe, C. (1977). *Friendly intruders.* Berkeley: University of California Press.

Katz, L. (1977). *Talks with teachers.* Washington, DC: National Association for the Education of Young Children.

Katz, M. (1971). *Class, bureaucracy and the schools.* New York: Praeger.

Kohl, H. (1967). *36 children.* New York: The New American Library.

Kohlberg, L., & Mayer, R. (1972). Development as the aim of education. *Harvard Educational Review, 42,* 449–496.

Larson, M. (1977). *The rise of professionalism.* Berkeley: University of California Press.

Lazerson, M. (1971). Social reform and early childhood education: Some historical perspectives. In R. Anderson & H. Shane (Eds.), *As the twig is bent* (pp. 22–33). Boston: Houghton Mifflin.

Levin, D. (1982). Moral education: The body's felt sense of value. *Teachers College Record, 84,* 283–301.

Lortie, D. (1975). *Schoolteacher.* Chicago: University of Chicago Press.

Macdonald, J. (1975). Curriculum and human interests. In W. Pinar (Ed.), *Curriculum theorizing: The reconceptualists* (pp. 283–294). Berkeley, CA: McCutchan.

Montessori, M. (1967). *The Montessori method* (A. George, Trans.). Cambridge, MA: Robert Bentley.

Oakes, J., Hare, S., & Sirotnik, K. (1986). Collaborative inquiry: A congenial paradigm in a cantankerous world. *Teachers College Record, 87,* 545–563.

Ozga, J., & Lawn, M. (1981). *Teachers, professionalism and class.* London: Falmer Press.

Pagano, J. (1985, October). *The claim of Philo.* Paper presented at the Bergamo Conference on Curriculum Theory and Classroom Practice, Dayton, OH.

Pestalozzi, J. (1907). *Leonard and Gertrude,* trans. Eva Channing. Boston: MA: D.C. Heath & Co.

Pinar, W. (1983). Curriculum as gender text: Notes on reproduction, resistance and male-male relations. *The Journal of Curriculum Theorizing, 5*(1), 26–53.

Porter, C. (1981). *Voices from the preschool: Perspectives of early childhood educators.* Unpublished doctoral dissertation, State University of New York at Buffalo.

Poulantzas, N. (1973). On social classes. *New Left Review, 78,* (March–April, 1973), 27–34.

Sarason, S. (1982). *The culture of the school and the problem of change.* Boston: Allyn & Bacon.

Seaver, J., & Cartwright, C. (1977). A pluralistic foundation for training early childhood professionals. *Curriculum Inquiry, 7,* 310–329.

Sergiovanni, T. (1985). Landscapes, mindscapes and reflective practice in supervision. *Journal of Curriculum and Supervision, 1*(1), 5–18.

Shakeshaft, C. (1986). Methodological issues in researching women in educational research: The legacy of a century. *Educational Researcher, 15*(6), 13–15.

Sharp, R., & Green, A. (1975). *Education and social control.* London: Routledge & Kegan Paul.

Silin, J. (1982). *Protection and control: Early childhood teachers talk about authority.* Unpublished doctoral dissertation, Teachers College, Columbia University.

Silin, J. (1986). Psychology, politics and the discourse of early childhood educators. *Teachers College Record, 87,* 611–618.

Silin, J. (1987). The early childhood educator's knowledge base: A reconsideration. In L. Katz (Ed.), *Current topics in early childhood education* (Vol. 7) (pp. 17–31). Norwood, NJ: Ablex.

Spodek, B. (1970). What are the sources of early childhood curriculum? *Young Children, 26*(1), 48–58.

Spodek, B. (1977). Curriculum construction in early childhood education. In B. Spodek & H. Walberg (Eds.), *Early childhood education: Issues and insights* (pp. 116–137). Berkeley, CA: McCutchan.

Spodek, B., & Saracho, O. (1982). The preparation and certification of early childhood personnel. In B. Spodek (Ed.), *Handbook of research in early childhood education.* New York: The Free Press.

Snyder, A. (1972). *Dauntless women in childhood education.* Washington, DC: Association for Childhood Education International.

Takanishi, R. (1981). Early childhood education and research: The changing relationship. *Theory into Practice, 20,* 86–93.

Tetreault, M., & Schmuck, P. (1985). Equity, educational reform, and gender. *Issues in Education, 3*(1), 45–68.

Tyack, D. (1974). *The one best system.* Cambridge, MA: Harvard University Press.

Tyack, D., & Hansot, E. (1982). *Managers of virtue.* New York: Basic Books.

Walsh, W. (1959). *The use of the imagination.* London: Chatto & Windus.

Weber, E. (1984). *Ideas influencing early childhood education.* New York: Teachers College Press.

Wright, E. (1976). Class boundaries in advanced capitalist societies. *New Left Review, 98* (July–August, 1976), 26–41.

Part III

TOWARD
DEVELOPING
PROFESSIONALISM

11 • Pathways to Professional Effectiveness for Early Childhood Educators

KAREN VANDER VEN
University of Pittsburgh

Professionalism in early childhood education refers to a wide array of professional knowledge and skills that impact on a similar range of needs of children, their families, and the societal systems that affect them. Since practitioners with these increasingly complex abilities only emerge over time, as a function of experience and ongoing development as adults, it is necessary for the field of early childhood education to recognize stages of development of professionalism among its practitioners.

This chapter describes a five-stage developmental sequence reflecting various levels of professionalism in early childhood educators as they actually practice in the field today. The large cadre of nonprofessionals currently practicing in early childhood programs requires that such a sequence acknowledge their presence by using nonprofessional practice as its baseline and by considering their relationship to the continued press to upgrade the quality of services provided by early childhood education.

This formulation not only will describe these five sequential stages as they relate to career path options in early childhood education, but also will identify the gaps and discontinuities in the professional continuum. This might then suggest ways of developing a more professional workforce in the future, one that can more powerfully and consistently meet the needs of young children and their families.

FACTORS IN THE DEVELOPMENT OF PROFESSIONALISM

Before the five stages of professionalism are presented, factors in the development of professionalism that provided a context for the model in the field of early childhood education will be discussed.

137

Professionalization
and Professionalism

Professionalization refers to the public recognition of and demand for a specialized service that can only be provided by people prepared to do it. To provide such services thus requires *professionalism*. Professionalism involves the utilization of special knowledge and skills that (1) are goal oriented and intended to achieve specific outcomes, (2) adhere to a standard of performance, and (3) require informed judgment to apply effectively (Katz, 1984b). To do the latter requires the ability to diagnose and analyze events, weigh alternatives, select the most appropriate intervention, apply it skillfully, and explain *why* it was selected. In sum, these qualities comprise *professional* practice.

In contrast, *nonprofessional* practice (Katz, 1984b) (1) reflects no particular knowledge or skill and (2) is *strongly* and *unmitigatedly* determined by past experience, personal values, and "common sense" (Vander Ven, 1980). These qualities are brought to bear to supply a quick and easy solution to the demands of the moment.

These concepts of professional and nonprofessional practice provide the basic theoretical framework for the foundation of the five stages presented in this chapter.

Roles and Functions
Required by the Field

To be a profession, a field must have a mission (Radomski, 1986); thus, development of professionalism in early childhood educators should be oriented toward their being able to address the field's basic mission of providing both education and caregiving from a developmental or (as appropriate) therapeutic perspective (Feeney & Chun, 1985; Logue, Eheart, & Levitt, 1986; NAEYC, 1984). Early childhood education in its broadest sense serves different functions: It can be delivered both directly (e.g., as clinical or "hands-on" work) and indirectly or contextually (e.g., as administration, advocacy, or research) (Vander Ven, 1981).

Thus, the five-stage formulation will show how development of professionalism is related to practitioner ability to assume the roles necessary to deliver the various functions of the field. Since levels of professionalism are related to the amount of direction or guidance required for practice, and since provision of this function is subsumed in the more advanced stages, the formulation will describe the nature of supervision at each stage.

Adult/Career Development

The fields of adult and career development provide an important supporting context for the consideration of the development of professionalism. The concept of adult development, as exemplified by the well-known formulations of persons such as Erikson (1950) and Levinson (1978, 1986), purports that growth in affect, cognition, and overall breadth of understanding and competence can take place throughout a lifetime, and that this development can be conceptualized in stages. That such development can be linked to increasing competence in careers is similarly supported by general theories of career development (Dalton, Thompson, & Price, 1977; Super & Hall, 1978). Within the field of education generally, and early childhood education specifically, formulations of stages of career development have been proposed (Burden, 1980; Frede, 1985; Katz, 1977; Siedow, 1985; Yarger & Mertens, 1980).

In line with these precedents for stage formulations of development, adult/career development is presented in stages, although many of the variables of practitioner growth are actually dimensions in a process of ongoing and gradual emergence toward greater recognition rather than discrete entities that suddenly arise and later disappear. The following four areas are cases in point that are of particular importance.

Adult cognition and affect. The ways practitioners think and feel about children, and the issues they confront in working with them, incisively influence the actual nature of their work. Thus a fundamental component of this formulation will be to show how shifts in practitioner cognition and affect over the course of adult development are related to the ability to deliver the various functions of early childhood education.

Lifelong careers. For achievement of the full professionalization of a field and the professionalism of its members, it would seem that it must offer options for lifelong careers in increasingly responsible functions in both direct and indirect practice, following the concept of full professionhood formulated by Etzioni (1969). Lifelong career options allow for ongoing retention of practitioners, thereby increasing representation in the field of persons who have had time to develop the advanced knowledge and skills that are the essence of the field's identity as a profession, and who can better contribute to the field's overall power and influence.

Men and women. There are differentials in the adult development and career status of men and women in early childhood education

(Acker, 1983; Seifert, 1985). While, in general, the global stages of adult development are quite similar for women and men (Stewart, 1977), within these there are some differences. For example, in Stewart's research on women utilizing the Levinson methodology, the greater variability in the ways in which women accomplish the four major stages of adult development is related to whether they choose primarily a marriage or a career focus to their lives in their twenties.

Midlife and post-midlife adult development. The midlife and post-midlife stages of adult development have been increasingly recognized as holding potential for professional achievement, particularly by women who at this time not only grow into awareness of their power and ability but also become more comfortable with assertiveness (Turbiner, 1982). Because these are qualities needed to address some of the most challenging issues in early childhood work, the potential of practitioners in later stages of development of professionalism to do so will be emphasized in the formulation.

The five-stage formulation proposed in this chapter will take these four issues into account in projecting the possibility for an entire working lifetime in early childhood education.

Direction of Practice

Another criterion for evaluating a profession is the ways in which the work of practitioners is guided, particularly at preprofessional levels. This is particularly important in a field that is not completely professionalized, that is, where practice is not autonomous. Thus the formulation will consider the functions of supervision and other forms of direction of practice, as the means for staff development and quality control, at the various stages.

Educational Preparation and Quality of Practice

Educational preparation of practitioners, specifically in early childhood and child development programs, is related to positive developmental outcomes for children (Ruopp, Travers, Glantz, & Coelen, 1979). This obviously makes a strong case for the field of early childhood education striving for professionalization, as well as for the contribution of education to professionalism. Thus the formulation will describe the levels of education associated with each stage of development of professionalism.

A FIVE-STAGE SEQUENCE OF DEVELOPMENT OF PROFESSIONALISM IN EARLY CHILDHOOD EDUCATORS

Stage 1: Novice

Level of professionalism. The term *novice* is used to refer to those numerous practitioners who fill subprofessional positions in programs delivering early childhood education. The most salient characteristic of novices is that they function as nonprofessionals, whether they are brand-new to the field or have been working for a number of years. This characterization is based on the fundamental premise that experience alone is not sufficient to provide professional competence. Nonprofessional behavior, in line with the earlier description, simply is that which is based on personal predilection and whatever seems to be the best way to deal with the perceived demands of a presented situation. Nonprofessional practitioners, as people, may range from the warm, kind, and well meaning—who in this way may inadvertently provide useful service—to those who in no way belong in early childhood education or in fact in any field in which there is direct contact with clients. This latter group may, at its extreme, include those relatively few who have performed blatant acts of abuse. Just as important, however, are those who, out of either ignorance or inappropriate personality attributes (e.g., the need to exercise authority), respond nonprofessionally to the situations they continually encounter in working with young children. As described by Katz (1984b), such persons may moralize, make threats, ignore, and use such exhortations as "Shut up," "Stop crying or I'll give you something to cry about," and others. They also may depersonalize or infantilize children in areas in which they should be encouraged to be autonomous: "Here, honey, I'll color that for you." This is an example of well-intentioned warmth not being in the educational or developmental interest of the child.

Roles and functions. This large group of novices, along with those in the next, or *initial* stage, is found primarily in direct-practice positions, both home based and center based, holding titles such as "assistant" or "aide." Thus the scope of their practice is within the immediate setting containing a child. In Bronfenbrenner's (1977) ecological hierarchy of systems affecting children, this is the microsystem, which includes the people, environment, activities, and arrangements of the setting. Novices' general role is to provide hands-on care, assist in the conduct of activities, manage behavior, and contribute to center maintenance. At the optimum, their presence contributes to service delivery by lowering the ratio of staff to children, which is related to developmental outcomes (Ruopp et al., 1979). In line with the function of the aide positions they often fill, these persons, by performing more routine duties, free more highly trained persons to use their skills.

Adult/career developmental stage. Persons functioning as professionals in a field usually enter it following a period of at least tentative career choice, followed by educational preparation for that field. Novices may fall into any age range; they are not necessarily only young people exploring career possibilities and/or formally preparing for them. Thus, they may fall into any established stage of adult/career development and may have negotiated these with varied degrees of successful outcome. It has been suggested that such persons have not completely resolved successfully the Eriksonian stages of identity and intimacy; it is gaps here in personal development that may prevent these persons from moving on to a higher level of professional growth (Tittnich, 1987).

Novices in positions working with young children receive income that serves as a source of maintenance. They may remain in the jobs on an ongoing basis or until something is found in another field. This is a totally respectable reason for working, of course, but it is more likely to be present in individuals who are more interested in getting by from day to day than in truly learning and growing into greater professional capacity. The fact that they are novices does not mean that at some time they will not shift into a position that engages them in a more legitimate commitment to work with children as a career, including embarking on a more formal process of professional development.

Cognitively, novices may be most likely to view practice in a concrete fashion; that is, they do not view behavior in terms of its developmental appropriateness and meaning. They usually do not seek likely causes within the context of a situation to explain occurrences and to suggest constructive ways of dealing with them. When they do, their thinking is apt to be *linear*, that is, seeing one singular variable as causing another (e.g., "Johnny is upset today because something is going on at home"), or patently *dichotomous*, that is, seeing things in an either/or perspective (e.g., "The children are playing, therefore they're not learning") (Vander Ven, in press).

Their view of issues and situations may be highly colored by their own personal experiences and value systems, a thought process that might be referred to as *personalization* (Johnson, 1985). In the absence of professional preparation, this is the major cognitive resource upon which they can rely. Thus, they will say, "This is the way I was treated when I was a child" (or "the way I raised my own children"); or, "All you need to work with children is common sense."

Direction of practice. Novices, obviously, require a high level of direction in their work. They are not always receptive to such supervision, for several reasons. The first is their commitment to the field, which is on the level of a job rather than a career. They are more likely to view supervision in a more negative sense, such as being "bossed" or controlled rather than as serving as a tool to them in their personal growth and professional progress. A second and legitimate factor may be their working conditions. They are on the lowest rung of the ladder, even in a comparatively "flat" organization, and this position is noted as being related to low morale. Similarly, low salaries, which may even be at the minimum-wage level, hardly serve to engage such practitioners into the additional investment necessary to assume a more professional orientation. There is a predominance of women in these positions, and they are more likely to accept low salaries and lack of benefits in return for the chance to work, possibly part time.

Level of educational preparation. Novices, in general, reflect the lowest legally permissible educational level at which a person may be hired in a caregiving position with children. This level ranges anywhere from eighth grade to high school graduation. Although they may have been exposed to mandated inservice training in their centers, their earlier school experiences may have caused them to be resistant to education. This encourages them also to reject the guidance of those who have had a higher level of formal education in the field. They justify their response on the premise that "you don't need a lot of book learning in order to work with children." These individuals have difficulty making applications of such material to their real-life practice; they are the ones who will sometimes say, when asked about the utility of a new approach, "We tried it and it didn't work."

Some novices who are more open to influence or who suddenly find an unexpected aptitude for early childhood work may be sufficiently transformed that they become receptive to educational activities and thus can make a transition to the next stage. But until external issues such as salary level and the general economic support base for early childhood education are addressed—events that would upgrade the qualifications for entry into early childhood education—the field will be confronted with the issues presented by a large nonprofessional workforce.

Stage 2: Initial

Level of professionalism.   Practitioners in the initial stage are differentiated from novices in that they have shown some formal commitment to developing a career in early childhood education. This is reflected by their involvement in some form of educational preparation for the work, albeit on a subprofessional level. Within this stage fall early childhood and child development students on fieldwork placement, persons perhaps working on their Child Development Associate credential or associate degrees; and persons who have completed formal inservice or paraprofessional training programs. In the broad sense these practitioners are conceptually unsophisticated, although they may have mastered some of the basic notions of developmental theory and have developed some skill in applied practice. As a result, their work may show a "flavor" of professionalism, but they may not be able to explain the reasons for what they do.

Roles and functions.   Practitioners in the initial stage, like novices, work essentially in the microsystem or immediate setting containing a child, such as a classroom or caregiving area. They provide both caregiving and educationally oriented activities, usually under assignment or close direction by a senior staff member. Promotion of *quality*, referring to those variables in practitioner behavior and the environment that encourage positive developmental outcomes (Curry, 1985), is a major microsystem issue. Initial-stage practitioners, with the knowledge and skill they do have, along, perhaps, with their greater investment and concern with what is appropriate practice, can make a supportive contribution to quality. They are more likely to show warm affect around their work, in line with the interesting finding that early childhood educators with some training are more likely to provide emotional warmth than are those who do not have any educational preparation (Feeney & Chun, 1985). However, they may also have a propensity to overdo their giving of themselves; Anna Freud's dynamic of "altruistic surrender" may apply, in which practitioners willingly sacrifice their own self-serving impulses to meet unswervingly the needs of others. It is reflected in the "rescue fantasy" phenomenon often observed as a developmental characteristic of entry-level workers in human service work. Behaviors such as overidentification with or attention to one child; gravitation toward particularly "needy" children; and difficulty in setting limits and denying children's requests often relate to practitioners' rescue fantasies. They may, however, contribute valued enthusiasm and spontaneity to their settings. The ultimate degree to which initial-stage practitioners can contribute to quality is probably highly dependent on the quality of the senior staff who supervise them and of the supervision itself.

Adult/career developmental stage. In general it is assumed that initial-stage practitioners fall into the young adult age range of 18 to 25, although there are exceptions, particularly among women reentering the workforce. The general theme displayed by persons in this stage seems well reflected in the concepts of *growing into adult work* (Levinson, 1978) and *apprenticeship* (Dalton, Thompson, & Price, 1977) as they work toward the completion of a qualification that will result in their entry into a formal career structure.

Initial-stage practitioners, because of their commitment and preliminary preparation, are more informed and less dogmatic in their thinking than novices. However, they still may tend to think of development and practice in a linear fashion, seeing one singular variable as causing another, particularly if the variables at hand are ones with which they are not highly familiar. Similarly, they may use a global concept to explain observed phenomena, such as, "The children are upset today because they are under so much stress." They may think dichotomously, as do novices, viewing various situations in either/or terms, such as, "That mother works, therefore she doesn't want to be with her child" (Vander Ven, 1984). Again, this is more likely to apply in areas of the field in which they have less experience, such as extended contact with parents.

These practitioners may think in a less personalized way than do novices, but they still may be driven by their own personal value systems about children and their needs. Such value systems can exert a strong influence on the form of practice of early childhood educators (Porter, 1980).

Persons who select work with other people often display a quality of "unproductive humility" (Vander Ven, 1984), which is the tendency to downplay their actual capabilities because "caring" people should be modest and self-effacing. This form of dichotomous thinking is quite likely to be observed in initial-stage practitioners. It may be accompanied by a generally passive stance and victimlike behavior; for example, initial-stage practitioners may see all the frustrations in their work as being caused by external forces about which they can do little.

Direction of practice. Initial-stage practitioners, like novices, require a high degree of direction in their work and by definition are closely supervised. But, in contrast, they generally are more receptive to such guidance. Being invested in the work, they actively look for prescriptions or methods that may help them to deal with the various challenging and ambiguous situations they encounter but do not yet have the cognitive ability or skills to confront completely. Furthermore, they may view supervision as the route to favorable recommendations, possible promotions, and as an overall support to development of a future career.

Level of educational preparation. Obviously initial-stage practitioners do not hold complete professional credentials for practice. Some may be actively participating in inservice training or working toward either a two- or four-year degree, or a Child Development Associate credential. In terms of the proposed NAEYC levels for educational preparation, these preprofessional practitioners fall at maximum into the category of early childhood teacher assistant.

Experience, personal development, ongoing training and education, and transition activities all will encourage initial-stage practitioners' growth into the next stage.

Stage 3: Informed

Level of professionalism. The third stage in the model, informed practice, is fulfilled by practitioners who have made a strong career commitment to the field, sufficient to enable them to complete a formal program of educational preparation that can be considered professional. At a minimum, this would be the baccalaureate level. Even though this would have included some direct, supervised experience that would provide skill development, substantial emphasis would be placed on theoretical and empirical information. Since informed practice is predicated on a specific knowledge base of developmental, psychological, and educational theory, and on a wide array of the skills that can be flexibly applied according to the demands of a situation, the stance of practitioners at this stage is most analogous to that of the "professional early childhood teacher" (Katz, 1984b).

One of the primary criteria differentiating informed-stage practitioners from those at the initial stage is the fact that they can rely on much more than common sense, their own childhood experience, and simplistic applications of basic empirical knowledge and theory. Still, they are not completely "seasoned" in terms of being able to deal with some of the more complicated demands of daily practice or with systematic variables that affect the delivery of direct service.

Roles and functions. Like their predecessors, informed-stage practitioners practice primarily in the *microsystem.* In this context, however, their increased knowledge, skill, and maturity allow them to address more precisely concerns related to *quality.* They are more likely, for example, to encourage children's thinking and problem solving by utilizing developmentally oriented methods that facilitate divergent thinking and avoid provision of information with the expectation of learner performance (Kamii, 1985). They are also more able to structure physical settings and activities in such a way as not only to reduce the need for external controls but also to work toward achievement of specific developmental goals. Similarly, they are able to respond more sensitively and empathically to children's affective expressions, utilizing both skill and understanding of development. They are able to provide goal-oriented activities with a specific purpose in mind, in contrast to the less sophisticated practitioner who does things more because the materials are there or because they will keep the children busy.

Practitioners in the informed stage may operate to some extent in the *mesosystem:* the network of systems containing children and the relationships among these systems (Bronfenbrenner, 1977). Mesosystem functions for the informed-stage practitioner include several major issues of concern to the early childhood field. One is the growing recognition of the need to work with the parents and families of children; another is obtaining and coordinating supplementary services for them. Here practitioners may begin to have considerable contact with parents, providing parent education, collaborating on developing consistent approaches to children, serving as positive role models for practice, and helping to assemble a cohesive package of supportive services from a diverse, although possibly inadequate, array of community offerings.

Adult/career developmental stage. Most practitioners in the informed stage have made a specific choice to prepare for and work in the early childhood field, by completing a program of educational preparation and thus specifically qualifying for a professional-level position. This would certainly represent some consolidation beyond Erickson's stage of identity; the practitioners may have made steps toward a transition to the intimacy stage. In so doing they make a shift from identification with childhood as a life stage to identification with parents and families as well. Often becoming parents themselves encourages a new form of empathy and concern for other parents. In general this step in personal development encourages practitioners to be able to take a broader perspective that allows them to address the kinds of mesosystem issues already described. As they accommodate to the demands of informed practice and begin to feel a part of a professional enterprise, practitioners correspondingly may be in a "settling-down" phase (Levinson, 1978). Some women, however, in line with Stewart's (1977) modification of Levinson's theory, may modify the intensity of their career pursuit by marrying and having a family. Those who enter standard full-time positions may now move from being apprentices to being *colleagues* (Dalton et al., 1977), where peer relationships and teamwork on the job become important factors in enriching performance and solidifying a sense of professional identity and commitment.

Informed-stage practitioners are moving away from linear and dichotomous thinking to what, indeed, might be called "flexible" thinking. Their perceptions, activities, and decisions are more likely to be based on real information rather than on subjective impressions, personal value systems, and past experiences. For example, rather than categorizing a particular approach, such as behavior modification, as "good" or "bad," they are able to evaluate it on the basis of actual knowledge and perhaps see both assets and liabilities in it.

The "unproductive humility" of the initial-stage practitioner begins to give way to more personal recognition of actual abilities and of the fact that a "victim" stance is singularly unproductive. Feeling more sure of their abilities, practitioners in the informed stage are also able to transform passivity into a more confident stance in which there is more ability to act to modify those external variables that do not positively support their work. For example, some at this stage may join their local professional associations and find out how they can be supportive in helping them to address issues of concern, such as program quality.

Direction of practice. These practitioners grow toward greater self-reliance in practice. They perform many daily activities without close supervision, although it is required for more complex situations they may confront. In line with their growing investment in the field, they may actively seek guidance for reasons of promoting their own personal and professional growth. By this time they are becoming more interested in dealing with contextual and systemic issues, in contrast to the initial-stage practitioner's greater interest in prescriptive solutions to concrete problems.

Level of educational preparation. Practitioners at the informed stage will have completed at minimum a baccalaureate level of education, most likely in child development or early childhood education. This supports the suggestion that has been made that the baccalaureate degree be the first level of preparation for the child-care fields (Principles and

Guidelines, 1982). Possession of the baccalaureate degree would presuppose acquisition of the theoretical and empirical knowledge that differentiates common sense and even hygienic (nonharmful) practice from that which is professional and informed. This corresponds to the third level of early childhood teacher in the NAEYC (1984) formulation.

Stage 4: Complex

Level of professionalism. The fourth stage, complex practice, is filled by practitioners who have accumulated some longevity in the field. In most cases they have progressed through the preceding stages so as to acquire the knowledge and experience necessary to pitch their service at a level that addresses increasingly more advanced or complicated problems and situations. Unlike the case with novices, in which experience alone does not necessarily improve quality of practice, experience for the professionally prepared early childhood educator can be integrated into an existing frame of reference and thereby serve to expand the practitioner's knowledge and competence. At this stage of professional development, two career path options become available: the direct-practice or clinical path and the indirect or contextual path involving such functions as supervision, administration, teaching other adults, advocacy, and research. Some may also follow a blended career path with both direct and indirect work, as in the case of the small-center director who also teaches three mornings a week (Vander Ven, 1980, 1981).

The dual career path options presented here represent an initial attempt to suggest a formulation of professional development in early childhood education that, by including both direct and indirect practice options, relates to the fact that a full-fledged profession must have options both for advanced clinical practice and for indirect work (Etzioni, 1969). In line with the general development of semiprofessions, it seems that early childhood has followed the path of developing indirect functions first. The direct-practice option, allowing for lifelong and increasingly complex and responsible practice, is now needed. The direct-practice option offered here is predicated on the premise that the knowledge and skills of early childhood educators can be applied in advanced ways to special situations and needs that transcend general group care for normal children.

Roles and functions. Stage 4 practitioners have the potential to make a massive contribution to addressing salient needs in the field.

Indirect practice. In an indirect capacity, complex-stage practitioners need to deal with the microsystem, the mesosystem, and the *exosystem*, to use Bronfenbrenner's (1977) four-tiered sequential hierarchy. The exosystem refers to those institutions of society—such as the economy, the mass media, the legislature, education, health care, housing, technology, and others—that incisively affect the nature and quality of life for children and families. It is well recognized that deficiencies in these areas are related to family difficulty and poor developmental outcomes (Bronfenbrenner, 1974). The activities of indirect practitioners, particularly, can be oriented toward addressing these areas, although this of course would be in a way circumscribed by the focus on the educational, care, and developmental needs of young children.

Economic issues, ranging all the way from the poverty experienced by large numbers of families (Washington & Oyemade, 1985) to the level of staff salaries in early childhood practice, must be directly addressed. Helping a parent find a job or develop a budget, developing a scale for salary increases for staff, and conceptualizing a new program model and applying for external funding are just a few examples of the economic aspects of early childhood work at the exosystem level. Issues related to family living conditions similarly fall within practitioners' purview at this stage; they may work with both individual families and the system as a whole, to gain appropriate health screening and care; transportation to center functions; and housing arrangements which, as much as possible, facilitate positive family life.

Technology, such as computers and telecommunications, is increasingly receiving attention from the human service disciplines for its ability to handle efficiently administrative components, to increase access to information, and to facilitate learning. However, technology's potential to impede or depersonalize human relationships is also recognized. Thus it becomes a concern for the early childhood educator at the complex stage, who knows how to utilize technology, to advance both managerial and direct service functions in the field without sacrificing the field's essential interpersonal component.

The educational system both for children and for personnel in the field (Almy, 1985) is also an exosystem issue. Although advances have been made in recent years in articulating and coordinating educational preparation for early childhood personnel, still more needs to be done in terms of adjusting educational levels and associated content and skills with needs in the field and effectively delivering these to practitioners. There is a need to ground the knowledge base more solidly in actual clinical experience (Silin, 1985). Well-qualified faculty in the academic sector are needed to develop this knowledge base (Peters, 1981). For children, the issue of early childhood's sponsorship within the service system is receiving major attention, as exemplified by the debate as to whether the public schools, with their emphasis on formal instruction, should also deliver early childhood services that require a developmental/caregiving approach (Blank, 1985).

Marketing and entrepreneurial activities are needed at this level to address the increasing need to promote assertively the public image of child care (Pettygrove, Whitebook, & Weir, 1984); to deliver services that are consumer, rather than provider, driven; to plan programs carefully to meet identified needs of target markets; and to work on the financial or business aspects of providing child care. Traditionally the entrepreneurially oriented component has been a weak aspect of early childhood education, due to practitioners' reluctance to become involved in such activities. It may take a more mature practitioner to see that taking a business-oriented stance is not alien to being a warm and caring service provider (Vander Ven, 1984).

Direct practice. There are many clinical problems requiring practitioners with advanced or clinical skills in direct work, meaning that they can view the problem in a complex context and bring to bear on it a variety of appropriate interventions. This is indeed the most complex and responsible form of direct work, blending caregiving, educational, and therapeutic roles together so that they can be utilized expansively according to the needs of the clients. In fact, it is the presence of caregiving and developmental aspects in a therapeutic function that makes the contribution of early childhood practitioners at this stage distinct from those of other disciplines that provide therapy, such as psychology and social work. For example, complex-stage practitioners might make particular use of play and activity media and the physical environment, in line with the emphasis on these as tools in early childhood work.

In the therapeutic role, the interventions provided may go beyond the behavioral level to address more in-depth or dynamic aspects of the children's or parents' personalities. A more intense interpersonal relationship may be formed in which transference elements may be present. Here the site of practice goes beyond the traditional group setting; these clinical early childhood educators may work in hospitals, clinics, mental health centers, and, in line with a growing trend, private practice.

Such practitioners may be involved in designing and conceptualizing programs of prevention and intervention that are targeted both toward specific clinical needs of a group and toward the system that contains it.

For example, the clinical perspectives of complex-stage practitioners can help enable special programing, such as mainstreaming, 24-hour care, or respite care, to be achieved positively.

Furthermore, the advanced knowledge and skills of persons at this stage can be utilized to address the needs of children and families in special situations, for example, assault, sexual abuse, divorce, disaster, and death; or with special populations characterized by one or even two forms of exceptionality, such as teenage parents or teenage parents of an exceptional child.

Adult/career developmental stage. The age range encompassed by practitioners at the complex stage is wide, as are the number and level of functions performed by them. The Eriksonian concept of *generativity*, which covers a large age span and describes the healthy adult's concern for development of the next generation, characterizes practitioners' adult development stage. Such concern is directly reflected in their commitment to the children and families with and for whom they work; and to the other adult practitioners whose development they facilitate so that these adults might provide more effective direct service. Their developmental stage also corresponds to Levinson's (1978) *becoming one's own person.* By the time practitioners have reached the complex-practice stage, they have probably made an ongoing commitment to a career in early childhood, not only having already amassed the experience and education needed to qualify them for more challenging modes of service, but also having survived the inherent barriers in early childhood careers, such as low pay.

Women in the older age range in which practitioners at the complex stage are found may have a particular potential to address the exosystem issues of advocacy that are so crucial for the field. Many women who previously may have been passive and nonassertive but who have negotiated the individuation process of midlife at this time may, as noted earlier (Turbiner, 1982), be feeling their real power for the first time, as well as being able to express strong feelings more directly. Both of these attributes are necessary in order to move recalcitrant systems. Since there are many women in early childhood, those who have progressed to this career stage should be able to form a constituency with ample "critical mass" to make an impact.

The demands made upon, and challenges facing, practitioners at the complex stage require a high level of cognitive and affective maturity. These individuals have moved incisively away from simplistic, linear thinking and now employ contextual or systems thinking in which they are "capable of seeing ordered patterns of relationship, processes, and interconnectedness in and between objects, phenomena, and people" (Duhl, 1983, p. 60). Such thinking is necessary to working within the varying aspects of the mesosystem and exosystem as well as with difficult clinical situations.

To select specific, sophisticated interventions appropriate for an intricate situation or to knowledgeably plan a complete program requires flexibility of thinking. Developmentally these practitioners have moved away from the initial need to have rigid rules and invariant prescriptions and can select interventions grounded in real client needs as seen in context with various systems.

The kind of goal-setting and proactive behavior required to provide the functions subsumed under the complex stage requires an instrumental stance; these practitioners are now able to base their activities on an assessment of future needs and the gathering of resources from the system in order to meet them.

Similarly, to obtain the services needed from various components of systems, it is necessary for practitioners to utilize an assertive stance in which, contrary to practitioners at preceding stages, they are actively able to ask for and work toward what they want for their clients and programs.

By this stage, unproductive humility has yielded to the marketing mentality needed to mount, comfortably and effectively, entrepreneurially oriented activities in which practitioners are able to ask for and command appropriate recognition for their accomplishments. This mental attribute is crucial for such activities as program design, public relations, and advocacy.

Direction of practice. Practitioners in the complex stage are able to act independently or autonomously, no longer requiring the close guidance or supervision needed in earlier stages. In fact, the ability to practice autonomously, particularly in a clinical function, is one of the characteristics of a fully professional practitioner (Etzioni, 1969).

Complex-stage practitioners are now the directors and supervisors of the practice of others at earlier stages of development of professionalism. Indeed, they may serve as mentors, in line with Dalton et al.'s (1977) stages of career development. The challenge for these practitioners, particularly those in administrative and supervisory positions, is to be able to deal effectively with the challenge presented by the novice practitioners. Furthermore, they may need to learn how to develop a support system; life for indirect practitioners in administrative positions can be lonely, as they may be the only ones in their setting holding such responsibilities. They may find such support among other practitioners who have begun to assume leadership roles, perhaps at the local level, as consultants, workshop leaders, or office holders in professional associations. In all of these roles they may have contact with younger practitioners for whom they serve as teachers and guides.

Level of educational preparation. Practitioners in the complex stage would most closely correspond educationally to the NAEYC's early childhood specialist, which requires an advanced degree or a baccalaureate degree plus experience. In this model for stages of professional development, however, it is suggested that the minimum requirement for practice at the complex stage be a graduate degree at the master's level; and that for certain activities, such as specialized clinical or therapeutic work and academic positions, preparation would be at the doctoral level.

Stage 5: Influential

Level of professionalism. Since no other models of professional development in early childhood or child care have dealt with the possibility of longevity in the field, this proposal for a stage of professionalism that relates to the maturity of older adults charts new territory, and hence will be more limited in its elaboration. Practitioners at the fifth or influential stage have had years of experience, served many roles and functions, and thus have an intimate and grounded grasp of the multifaceted aspects of the field. It should be pointed out that not everyone who enters early childhood work, or even remains in it until retirement, will reach the influential stage. But as early childhood education continues to develop, gradually offering increased opportunity and options, it can be expected that more and more people may come to hold such a position.

Roles and functions. The activities of influential-stage practitioners could touch all four levels of the Bronfenbrenner (1977) hierarchy, but those in the exosystem and macrosystem would be emphasized. In fact, probably only the most wise and mature practitioners are capable of serving a macrosystem function, the macrosystem being the overarching values and structures of society as they affect the lives of children and families. To transform these pervasive, embedded attitudes generally requires the collective synergism from energetic, targeted efforts in areas embraced by Bronfenbrenner's other three levels. It is this that can allow for prevention and modification of the conditions that contribute to such problems as poverty, child abuse, and teenage pregnancy. Occasionally an individual serves as a truly.transformational force, but those who have indeed been so influential as to be able to change macrosystem attitudes or structures are rare. Some may now be emerging into this capacity following highly successful and complex professional careers in the field. Such experience has allowed them to develop the wisdom and vision necessary to have an impact on the macrosystem.

In a more concrete fashion, such individuals may hold such positions as senior faculty in academic settings; as heads of national, regional, and state offices concerned with children and child welfare; as senior office holders in national organizations; and as directors of well-known, model service programs. Most actually hold composite roles; that is, they may engage in more than one form of activity. They may direct and on occasion even provide direct service in programs serving children and families; they may teach other adults, hold major organizational offices, perform research, and publish professionally.

Adult/career developmental stage. Ages of practitioners in the influential stage may range from midlife through post-midlife, preretirement, and even postretirement. Some may be at the height of their careers. Others, growing older, may have begun a reduction of physical activity without loss of their mental powers, in line with the notion that, while late adulthood can be a time of decline, it can as well be an "opportunity for development" (Levinson, 1978, p. 37). In the Eriksonian schema, some will still be in the stage of *generativity*, while those who are older will have accomplished the transition to *integrity*, in which they have a sense of positive accomplishment on behalf of others and know that they have an experienced voice that should inform other professionals and the public. It is hoped they will have the kind of support system that will provide them with the respect and real logistical assistance that will allow them to use their best thinking to the maximum. Such individuals will be sponsors, in line with the formulations of Dalton et al. (1977); these are people with creative ideas who have the ability to shape things.

Wisdom is becoming an important construct in contemporary adult psychology. Concomitantly it is becoming more recognized as a valued capacity in older adults (Holiday & Chandler, 1986). In this context, wisdom includes the exceptional understanding of ordinary experience; judgment and communication skills, such as the ability to consider options and various points of view; and interpersonal skills. Influential-stage practitioners in early childhood education have developed these capacities and utilize them in the complete array of their activities.

Practitioners at the influential stage have already developed competence in all of the other roles in early childhood education and thus have a wealth of experience, knowledge, and advanced thought to bring to their function at this stage. Their activities are in a reflective mode, by which they show their concern and dedication for the field by looking at its complexities and needs in a way that may generate new and creative perspectives. These can be communicated to others and utilized to guide the field's future development.

Such practitioners have developed the most advanced ways of thinking and feeling about concerns and issues in the field. Their thinking has come a long way from the linear and dichotomous approaches of the initial-stage practitioner; now they are able to think synergistically (King, 1975), being able not only to conceptualize systems but to unite apparently diverse concepts at a higher level of abstraction. This kind of creativity is essential to developing new, exciting, and powerful ways of looking at problems and challenges of the field.

In selecting activities and interventions, they are able to take an embracing view of a wide array of possibilities and from them select those that will be the most effective.

These practitioners also have come a long way from the passive stance of those at the initial stage; at the influential stage their approach is proactive. In a forward way, they identify needs and marshall forces to meet them before the conditions causing them become highly entrenched.

Going beyond even a marketing mentality, these practitioners are quite comfortable with promotion, quite forthrightly stating their positions, their needs, and their abilities, if they feel that doing so may benefit their constituencies in the field.

Finally, their experience allows them a high level of autonomy. Not only can they practice without supervision, but in fact their leadership ability makes them pacesetters for others at earlier stages of professional development.

Direction of practice. By definition, influential-stage practitioners are self-directed. Other practitioners and the field as a whole rely on them for overall guidance, direction, and leadership. A particularly salient feature of their approach is that they do not apologize for or hesitate to provide their perspectives. Unlike practitioners at earlier levels, who have responsibility for other staff, they are not conflicted or ambivalent about assuming authority. Unfortunately for all, sometimes a regressive component of individuals and groups who do not like to see change or progress, and who resist those who promulgate it, may pose some negative challenge to forward-looking influential-stage practitioners.

Level of educational preparation. Practitioners in the influential stage may demonstrate a range of educational preparation, from minimal to advanced, although it would be most likely that they have completed a doctorate, if only because many positions in the field that carry with them power and influence require a doctoral degree as a qualification. At this stage, however, quality and breadth of experience, along with personality characteristics, transcend the effects of formal preparation. Formally recommended guidelines for levels of educational preparation presently do not address practitioners in the influential stage, but probably educational programs at all levels should encourage students to aspire to the highest level of practice and identify the possibilities.

CONCLUSION

This chapter has presented a five-stage formulation of the process of development of professionalism in early childhood educators, beginning by necessity with a sub- or nonprofessional level of practice. It is suggested that this formulation be viewed as an initial step in the identification of stages of professionalism over a possible lifelong career trajectory in the field.

As the formulation is reviewed, it will be obvious that there are major gaps and discontinuities in the development of professionalism vis-à-vis today's workforce in early childhood education. This is particularly apparent for the large novice-stage group, whose members provide a great amount of direct service but whose potential for professional growth is in many instances modest. Similarly, initial-, informed-, and complex-stage practitioners with growth potential must be sustained in the field by adequate salaries and educational and career-ladder possibilities. Every attempt should be made to utilize the wisdom of influential-stage practitioners to solve the problems that hinder the development of professionalism—and hence the professionalization—of early childhood education. Particularly useful here would be the midlife and post-midlife energy and growing assertiveness of the women in the field.

Other future endeavors might include conceptualization of a formal model based upon empirical data, and proposals for specific transition activities that will facilitate smooth movement from one stage to another. Most important, however, is the transformation of the political/economic base of care and education for children, such that the first level of professionalism could begin at a true professional baseline. This is a fundamental way of addressing the growing concern for the total quality of service provided for young children and their families.

REFERENCES

Acker, S. (1983). Women and teaching: A semi-detached sociology of a semi-profession. In S. Walker & L. Barton, (Eds.), *Gender, class and education.* London: Falmer.

Blank, H. (1985). Public policy report. Early childhood and the public schools: An essential partnership. *Young Children, 40*(4), 52–55.

Bronfenbrenner, U. (1974). *A report on longitudinal evaluations of preschool programs* (DHEW Publication No. OHD 76-30025). Washington, DC: U.S. Government Printing Office.

Bronfenbrenner, U. (1977). Towards an experimental ecology of human development. *American Psychologist, 32,* 513–530.

Burden, P. (1980). Teachers' perceptions of the characteristics and influences on their personal and professional development (ERIC Document No. ED 198-087). Urbana, IL: Educational Resources Information Clearinghouse.

Curry, N. (1985). A developmental perspective on practice. In L. Schweinhart & D. Weikart (Eds.), *Quality in early childhood education programs: Four perspectives.* Ypsilanti, MI: High/Scope Educational Research Foundation.

Dalton, G., Thompson, P., & Price, R. (1977, Summer). The four stages of professional careers—A new look at performance by professionals. *Organizational Dynamics,* pp. 19–42.

Duhl, B. (1983). *From the inside out and other metaphors.* New York: Brunner/Mazel.

Erikson, E. (1950). *Childhood and society.* New York: W.W. Norton.

Etzioni, A. (Ed.). (1969). *The semi-professions and their organization.* New York: Free Press.

Feeney, S., & Chun, R. (1985). Research in review: Effective teachers of young children. *Young Children, 41*(1), 47–52.

Frede, E. (1985). How teachers grow: Four stages. In *High/Scope Resource.* Ypsilanti, MI: High/Scope Educational Research Foundation.

Holiday, S., & Chandler, M. (1986). *Wisdom: Explorations in adult competence.* Basel, Switzerland: Karger.

Johnson, C. (1985). *An extension of models of parent conceptions of child development to the case of child care.* Unpublished manuscript, University of Pittsburgh, Pittsburgh, PA.

Kamii, C. (1985). Leading primary education towards excellence: Beyond worksheets and drill. *Young Children, 40*(6), 3–11.

Katz, L. (1977). *Talks with teachers.* Washington, DC: National Association for the Education of Young Children.

Katz, L. (1984a). *More talks with teachers.* Urbana, IL: Educational Resource Information Clearinghouse.

Katz, L. (1984b). The professional early childhood teacher. *Young Children, 39*(5), 3–11.

King, M. (1975). *For we are.* Reading, MA: Addison-Wesley.

Levinson, D. (1978). *The seasons of a man's life.* New York: Alfred A. Knopf.

Levinson, D. (1986). A conception of adult development. *American Psychologist, 41*(1), 3–13.

Logue, M., Eheart, B., and Leavitt, R. (1986). Staff training: What difference does it make? *Young Children, 41*(5), 8–9.

National Association for the Education of Young Children. (1984). *Early childhood teacher education guidelines for four and five year programs.* Washington, DC: National Association for the Education of Young Children.

Peters, D. (1981). Up the down escalator: How to open the door. Comments on professionalism and academic credentials in child care. *Child Care Quarterly, 10*(3), 261–269.

Pettygrove, W., Whitebook, M., & Weir, M. (1984). Beyond babysitting: Changing the treatment and image of child care givers. *Young Children, 39*(5), 14–21.

Porter, C. (1980). *Voices from the preschool: Perspectives of early childhood educators.* Unpublished doctoral dissertation, State University of New York at Buffalo.

Principles and guidelines for child care personnel preparation programs. Proceedings of the Conference on Research Sequence in Child Care Education, University of Pittsburgh. (1982). *Child Care Quarterly, 11*(3).

Radomski, S. (1986). Professionalization of early childhood educators: How far have we progressed? *Young Children, 41*(5), 20–23.

Ruopp, R., Travers, J., Glantz, F., & Coelen, C. (1979). *Children at the center: Summary findings and their implications. Final Report of the National Day Care Study.* Cambridge, MA: Abt Associates.

Seifert, K. (1984, April). *The achievement of care: Men who care for young children.* Paper presented at the annual conference of the American Educational Research Association, New Orleans, LA.

Seifert, K. (1985, March). *Career experiences of men who teach young children.* Paper presented at the Annual Conference of the American Educational Research Association, Chicago, IL.

Siedow, M. (1985). Selecting presentation methods and staff. In M. Siedow, D. Memory, & P. Bristow (Eds.), *Inservice education for content area teachers.* Newark, DE: International Reading Association.

Silin, J. (1985). Authority as knowledge: A problem of professionalization. *Young Children, 40*(3), 41–46.

Stewart, W. (1977). *A psychosocial study of the formation of the early adult life structure in women.* Doctoral dissertation, Columbia University, New York, NY. Dissertation Abstracts International.

Super, D., & Hall, D. (1978). Career development: Exploration and planning. *Annual Review of Psychology, 29,* 333–372.

Tittnich, E. (1987, February). Personal communication to Karen Vander Ven.

Turbiner, M. (1982). *An empirical phenomenological investigation of the experience of self for adult females.* Unpublished doctoral dissertation, University of Pittsburgh, Pittsburgh, PA.

Yarger, S., & Mertens, S. (1980). Testing the waters of school based teacher education. In D. Corrigan & K. Howey, (Eds.), *Special education in transition.* Reston, VA: Council for Exceptional Children.

Vander Ven, K. (1980). A paradigm describing stages of personal and professional development of child care practitioners with characteristics associated with each stage. In *Proceedings of the Ninth International Congress of the International Association of Workers with Maladjusted Children* (pp. 111–126). Montreal, Canada: International Association of Workers with Maladjusted Children.

Vander Ven, K. (1981). Patterns of career development in group care. In F. Ainsworth & L. Fulcher, (Eds.), *Group care for children: Concept and issues.* London: Tavistock.

Vander Ven, K. (1984). Barriers to an effective marketing stance in child care. *Journal of Children in Contemporary Society, 17*(2), 43–56.

Vander Ven, K. (in press). How adults think about children: A significant variable in their development and potential well-being. *Proceedings of the 1984 20th Anniversary Conference of the Pittsburgh Association for the Education of Young Children.* Pittsburgh: Pittsburgh Association for the Education of Young Children.

Washington, V., & Oyemade, U. (1985). Changing family trends: Head Start must respond. *Young Children, 40*(6), 12–19.

12 • Implicit Theories of Early Childhood Teachers: Foundations for Professional Behavior

BERNARD SPODEK
University of Illinois

To be a professional teacher is to be an effective teacher. While we often discuss professionalism in terms of entry requirements, levels of preparation, codes of ethics, and other such attributes, these are essentially indicators of effectiveness. But what does it take to be an effective teacher of young children? To learn this, researchers in the field have studied teachers and their teaching over the decades.

It is generally believed that the more we know about teaching, the better able we will be to improve teachers' effectiveness and thus influence the educative process. In addition, it has been thought, knowledge of the nature of teaching would provide the basis for improving the preparation of teachers. To that end, there have been innumerable studies of teachers in action. Many of the early studies of teachers have focused on their personal characteristics. The assumption has been that individual personality variables translate directly or indirectly into good teacher performance. Other studies have focused on teacher behaviors. The assumption underlying these studies has been that the competence and effectiveness of a teacher can be determined by what that teacher does. It was felt that the key to understanding the nature of teaching could be found by observing what teachers do as well as what they are. Once we could determine those behaviors that characterize good teachers, we could train novices in these behaviors to prepare them as competent teachers.

There is more to teaching than observable actions, however. Even when teachers are visibly inactive and not manifesting any external behaviors, they may be functioning as teachers. They could be reflecting on what has taken place in the classroom or thinking ahead about what they wish to happen and how they might make it happen in the future. Teachers consistently process information gained from observing what takes place prior to, during, and after their decision making, as well as the actions they take based on the decisions made. They project a future based upon knowledge gained from past experience. In addition, teachers function in a consistent way, so one can anticipate how a particular teacher will function at different times and in different settings.

Teachers process the information they collect as they work with children. They come to understand the meaning of this information in relation to the educational concepts and values they have accumulated. Teachers' actions and classroom decisions are driven by their perceptions, understanding, and beliefs. They create conceptions of their professional world based upon their concept of that reality. These conceptions provide a way to interpret their perceptions in terms of their beliefs about what is true. These interpretations, in turn, become the basis for teachers' decisions and actions in the classroom. In order to understand the nature of teaching, one must understand not only the behavior of the teachers observed but also the teachers' thought processes regarding teaching and the conceptions that drive these processes.

TEACHERS' IMPLICIT THEORIES

The implicit theories, constructs, or belief systems, as they have been variously called, underlying early childhood educational practice have been of interest to a number of scholars over the years and have been studied in a number of ways (cf. Spodek, 1987; Spodek & Rucinski, 1984). Basil Bernstein (1975) has studied the beliefs underlying early childhood programs in England. He suggests that an invisible pedagogy underlies English infant schools, which serve children ages five through seven. This pedagogy is consistent with the style of middle-class mothering but is in conflict with that of working-class mothering. Thus, the infant school legitimizes the middle-class child's home experience while creating discontinuity and conflicts with that of the working-class child. The type of education that teachers have been creating in these schools results from the teachers' ideologies, that is, their views of what is good for children as well as what is educationally effective.

In a similar tradition, Michael Apple and Nancy King (1977) argue that schools in America have been used to collect and distribute particular social and economic meanings (forms of knowledge) to children. These social meanings reflect the ideologies of school life, which in turn reflect the ideologies of middle-class society. Apple and King examined the relationship between societal values and purposes and the culture of a kindergarten classroom, as well as the underlying meanings of classroom activities. According to these authors, as children enter the kindergarten, they are required to accommodate to the school setting. Their teachers are concerned with socializing them to fit into the existing social structure. They teach the children to share, to listen, to put things away, and to follow directions. The children are required to conform, to be quiet, and to be cooperative. Early in the year, children learn to make the important distinction between work and play. Work is seen as something that they must do, while play is seen is something that they can do. The children also learn to respond to the power of the teacher, a lesson that serves them well throughout their school careers. Like Bernstein, Apple and King view teachers' ideas and beliefs as well as the actions they govern as being political and ideologically driven. Thus, the forms of education provided, as well as the teaching practices, reflect assumptions about what children and teachers should do in a school situation.

In examining the ideologies of English infant teachers, Ronald King (1978) analyzed the cognitive constructs (i.e., beliefs, values, and behavioral customs) that these teachers imparted to young children through the school. He found that infant school teachers manifested a child-centered ideology, which was related to such basic concepts as developmentalism, individualism, play as learning, and childhood innocence. These ideological elements were instrumental in helping teachers construct a conception of a learning environment. What these infant school teachers believed about children and the learning process was integral to what happened in classrooms.

Young children were viewed as passing through a naturally ordered sequence of physical, psychological, and social development, although each child's individuality was also recognized. Young children were also seen as curious, wishing to explore the world around them, and learning best through play when they were happy, busy, and able to choose from activities of interest to them. The teachers functioned to create conditions that would help children develop to their highest individual potential.

In their thinking about children, Ronald King's (1978) teachers typified each individual in ways that explained variant behavior and determined how teachers would act to help children. Boundaries defining subject areas were blurred, as was the distinction between work and play. Certain distinctions were made, however, about play, which was viewed as (1) a prelude to work, (2) a form of learning, (3) a reward for working, and (4) a chosen activity. Work, on the other hand, was (1) defined by the teacher, (2) done for the teacher, (3) done in the morning, (4) an activity that could not be refused, and (5) an activity whose completion was defined by the teacher. These concepts, because they were shared by teachers, led to a consistency in school practice.

Berlak, Berlak, Bagantos, and Midel (1975) also studied the constructs, values, and beliefs of English infant school teachers. These teachers were involved in setting work requirements, motivating individual children, and establishing standards of performance. In observing and interviewing teachers, the authors noted that teachers' actions were often driven by conflicting values and constructs. Rather than respond to a consistent set of values, these teachers often held contradictory values. Thus, their decisions took the form of resolving dilemmas, often in terms of particular situations. What might seem like inconsistent responses on the part of the teachers came to be viewed as more rational and professional responses when viewed in the context of the dilemmas faced.

George Kelly (1955) uses the notion of personal construct to explain the way in which individuals construe things as being alike or different from each other. He suggests that each person's construct system is composed of a finite number of dichotomous constructs which are useful in anticipating events, allowing the individual to predict, manage, and control events to varying degrees. Each person actively constructs a representation of aspects of reality as a result of experiencing and interpreting events. These constructs precede actions and help determine what actions to take. Persons revise their constructs as they take into account feedback from their environment.

Bussis, Chittendon, and Amarel (1976) applied Kelly's (1955) notion of personal constructs to the study of teachers' professional understanding. Bussis et al. (1976) used this idea of personal constructs to understand teachers' representations of educational contexts and the consequences of those representations as translated into classroom actions. This was done by extrapolating the idea of the teacher's curriculum construct from Kelly's (1955) notion of personal construct. The researchers (Bussis et al., 1976) interviewed kindergarten, first-, and second-grade teachers regarding their classroom practices. These responses were then analyzed and put into categories representing curriculum, understanding of children, perceptions of the working environment, and perceptions of support from advisers (project supervisors). The teachers were then asked to confirm or disconfirm the portrayal of their constructs by the researchers. This resulted in the identification of the teachers' curriculum construct systems, which are analogous to the implicit theories of teachers studied by other researchers.

Gail Halliwell (1980), building on this work, studied the curriculum constructs of three kindergarten teachers. She found that these kindergarten teachers responded to their individual, professional perceptions of the needs of children in their classes. The teachers characterized the children as having individual growth patterns, interests, and learning modes. One of the teachers in the study focused heavily on mainstreaming handicapped children in her classroom. She showed particular interest in these children's participation and in their sense of success. Her teaching priorities included helping children to enjoy school, get along with others, and experience academic growth. The second kindergarten teacher wanted her program to be predictable for children, yet flexible and responsive to individual interests. Her teaching priorities included helping children to get along with one another and to develop thinking skills in academic areas. The third kindergarten teacher wanted her teaching to encourage children's concern for themselves and others. She also wanted them to feel responsible for their own learning and to develop academically. These teachers' constructs illuminated the reasons for their own professional actions and for the development of particular activities and interactions in their respective classrooms. Thus, the consistency of teaching practice in each of these classes could be understood in terms of each teacher's particular curriculum constructs.

More recently, Margaret Yonemura (1986) studied one early childhood teacher. Through a combination of classroom observations and discussions, she came to understand the ideas, values, and beliefs of that teacher, how they were put into practice, and the meaning they had in the experience of the children. The teacher's professional beliefs related to the children she taught—their needs, capacities, motivations, feelings, autonomy, and initiative. They also related to the teacher's classroom functioning, including sharing decision making; balancing the needs of individuals against those of the group; disciplining children; and respecting the importance of formal knowledge, play, and children's experience.

Yonemura's (1986) description of the beliefs of the teacher showed a balance of professional values and technical concerns underlying the teacher's classroom practices. The teacher's personal knowledge was as important to her professional practice as was her technical knowledge of teaching. By becoming aware of these ideas, values, and beliefs, one could understand the underlying basis of competent teaching (i.e., teaching at a highly professional level) for this one individual.

In each of the studies reviewed here, the teachers' thought processes determined the actions that were taken in the classroom. It provided for an interpretation of events and a way of predicting the consequences of teachers' actions. It established the foundation for teachers' professional behavior. This is consistent with Argyris and Schön's (1975) conception of "theories-in-use." These theories undergird professional practice. They are not those developed by scholars and tested through research. Rather, they are developed by professional practitioners out of the distillation of their experience and the experience of others and are tested in the crucible of clinical practice. These theories provide the basis for interpreting experience and help determine the decisions and actions of practitioners.

ANALYZING EARLY CHILDHOOD TEACHERS' IMPLICIT THEORIES

A line of research has been developing regarding the thought processes of classroom practitioners. Such studies have been summarized by Clark and Yinger (1979), who have organized their review of research around the topics of *planning, judgment, interactive decision making,* and *teachers' implicit theories.* A more recent review of research on teachers' thought processes was presented by Clark and Peterson in 1986. They reviewed studies of *teacher planning, teachers' interactive thoughts and decisions,* and *teachers' theories and beliefs.* In this latter area, Spodek (1987) and Spodek and Rucinski (1984) studied the educational beliefs, or implicit theories, of early childhood teachers, relating their classroom work to the theories-in-use that underlie their classroom decisions. They addressed the following questions:

1. Is there a system of professional teacher constructs, theories, or beliefs that can be identified in early childhood teachers?
2. To what role dimensions are the identified constructs or theories related?
3. Are there patterns of individual variability of constructs or theories that can be found among teachers?
4. Do such patterns provide a consistent profile for individual teachers?

In analyzing the implicit theories of these early childhood teachers, a number of interesting findings were evident. Few of the teachers' implicit theories were shared by all, even among teachers working with children of the same age. Rather, individual teachers had diverse sets of implicit theories. Two of the first-grade teachers shared many implicit theories, as did two kindergarten teachers. Two of the preschool teachers also shared a number of theories. The kindergarten teachers had similar forms of professional preparation, having degrees in education. The two preschool teachers, however, had quite different preparation, one in an education program and the other in a child development program; and yet the principles upon which they based their classroom decisions were often the same. Thus, rather than being able to identify the implicit theories that might underlie professional practice for early childhood teachers in general, it was found that the theories held were personal in nature, even though they were related to professional actions.

The bulk of these early childhood teachers' implicit theories were related to keeping the class going and fell into the categories of *classroom management, instructional processes,* and *planning and organization* (Spodek, 1987; Spodek & Rucinski, 1984). In addition, the preschool teachers articulated many theories related to supporting play activities, which, at this level, is considered one of the prime ways that children learn. In contrast, the kindergarten teachers, responsible for socializing children into the elementary school, expressed many theories about their children's behavior. First-grade teachers, whose children have already entered the formal part of the elementary school, held theories that focused more on their children's learning.

The teachers' decisions were driven as much by value-oriented theories as by technical theories. Such value-oriented implicit theories are not easily modified by the results of research or by new educational or developmental theories. This reflects the difficulty that reformers have in modifying teachers' classroom practices by recourse to the results of research.

Another interesting finding (Spodek, 1987; Spodek & Rucinski, 1984) was the absence of implicit theories relating to evaluation among the preschool teachers studied and the absence of theories relating to play and children's characteristics among the primary teachers. Perhaps preschool teachers are less concerned with evaluation than are teachers at other levels of education. They did, however, reflect a concern for helping children adapt to the group and become involved in classroom activities.

It is evident from some of the studies cited earlier (e.g., Apple & King, 1977; Halliwell, 1980) that by the end of kindergarten the children are socialized to be aware of the distinction between work and play, and that work takes on a more central role in the classroom than does play. This could explain the absence of a focus on play in the theories of these kindergarten and primary teachers. The absence of stated theories at the first-grade level regarding children's characteristics might also reflect the shift from the child-centered programs of the preschool/kindergarten to the content-centered programs of the elementary school.

FOUNDATIONS FOR PROFESSIONAL PRACTICE

Professional practice in early childhood education consists of highly competent, rationally based teaching, along with the nonclassroom activities in which teachers engage. The fact that so many of the implicit theories underlying the teachers' classroom decisions are value oriented and concerned with managing classroom activities seems to raise issues about the foundations for professional practice in early childhood education. For a long time, many early childhood educators viewed the field as a practical application of the scientific field of child development (Caldwell, 1984). It was assumed that providing increased knowledge of child development research and theory would improve the work of classroom teachers. It has been argued that the professionally trained preschool teacher makes classroom decisions based upon "the most reliable knowledge about the development of children; the norms of the age group; and the goals of the parents, the school, and the community at large" (Katz, 1984, p. 29).

However, teachers don't seem to refer to developmental theory when they are making classroom decisions, but rather depend on theories they have developed as much from practical experience as from the formal knowledge they have gained in their preparation. While the teachers studied considered goals or values in their classroom decisions, we have no information as to whose goals were actually reflected. There was great diversity in the values reflected in their decisions, in spite of the fact that they all came from the same larger community and two of them came from the same school. This would suggest that the goals were more personal than school or community based. In addition, relatively few of the teachers' implicit theories were grounded in reliable knowledge of child development and learning theory. Instead, the teachers' decisions were often opportunistic and seemed to be rooted in a form of personal practical knowledge (Connelly & Clandinin, 1984; Elbaz, 1983).

In an attempt to test this idea, the categorized belief statements of the two kindergarten teachers were sent to 10 child development specialists at institutions such as the University of Delaware, University of Illinois, University of Michigan, University of Minnesota, Northern Illinois University, and Purdue University. They were asked if they could identify the principle from child development theory or research that was reflected in each implicit theory statement. Two sets of statements were returned immediately with the recipients writing that they would not have the time to meet this request in a reasonable period. A third specialist called and asked if there could be more time given to complete the task than was provided by the original suggested deadline. It should be noted that the task turned out to be much more time consuming and complicated than originally imagined; months later, the set of statements still had not been returned.

A fourth response was received, the only one that included a returned list, as of this writing. The specialist, a professor in a midwestern university, had passed the task on to a graduate student, who also begged off because of the lack of time. The list was finally responded to by a teacher in the laboratory nursery school, who identified the general theory that she felt was related to the teacher statements. This task alone, it was noted, took four hours.

While this experience might not be considered a reliable test of the relationship of formal child development theory to teachers' implicit theories, it does indicate that knowledge of child development research and theory might not be easily accessible, even to highly sophisticated child development specialists, let alone classroom teachers. Certainly a classroom teacher operating in a room with as many as two dozen children does not have the time to reflect on these scholarly principles before making a judgment. If, indeed, the teachers in the studies by Spodek and his colleagues (1984, 1985)—all well-educated, experienced professionals—did make use of this form of technical knowledge, then it must have been transformed in some way and been internalized to be easily accessible. Whether that is indeed the case is not known, nor do we know by what mechanism such a transformation of knowledge might take place.

How can we determine what actually is the knowledge base of the professional practice of early childhood education? While child development theory and learning theory are certainly elements in that base, they apparently are not directly accessible to teachers as they function with children in the classroom. This does not mean that child development theory is not useful or even necessary to the practice of early childhood education. Such theory provides both the basis and rationale for professional actions. But it is plausible that teachers transform this knowledge as they work with children. The transformation occurs as child development theory is integrated with other elements to make a set of theories that drive professional teaching acts.

Barbara Biber (1984) also raises the issue of using developmental theory as a foundation for early childhood professional practice. She has questioned whether there is a body of theory that is sufficiently comprehensive to be the foundation for educational practice. She suggests that psychological theories need to be less insulated from their practical application. She also suggests that theories need to be more comprehensive, possibly through the combination of theories that differ in substantive ways but have a common ideological base.

Developmental theory, however, no matter how comprehensive, cannot adequately serve as the sole theoretical basis for early childhood practice. In looking at the teachers' implicit theories, one can identify at least two additional elements—values and knowledge of practice—both of which need to be included in the foundation of early childhood professional practice. Indeed, about half of the teachers' implicit theories identified in the Spodek (1987) study were statements of value, dealing with what children "ought to be and become," as Biber (1984, p. 303) has so nicely phrased it, or with what teachers ought to do or be, these latter being essentially statements of professional ethics. These elements are very important, since education is essentially an ethical act, concerned with changing children and in some way making them better.

Teachers' knowledge of practice, the third foundational element of professional practice, includes five content areas: curriculum, subject matter, instruction, milieu, and self (Elbaz, 1983). Generated from a view of secondary teaching, these content areas are also a concern of early childhood teachers. The awareness of all these areas is what allows the professional teacher to orchestrate all the elements in an educational setting to facilitate learning in children. Because these elements are absent from developmental theory, they need to be integrated with it, within a value orientation.

Teachers' practical knowledge should not be disregarded because it is not formally generated and tested by research. While it is intuitive, it is derived from the experience of teachers and validated within the context of daily practice. Because it is so personally meaningful, growing out of experience and one's interpretations of those experiences, each teacher evolves his or her own personal conceptions to be applied, along with the other foundational aspects, to an understanding of the educational context. Thus the foundation for early childhood professional practice is created.

CONCLUSION

The study of teachers' thought processes is still relatively new. We still do not know how all teachers think about all aspects of professional practice. We still do not understand a great deal about how teachers develop their own implicit theories of education or about the impact of these theories on practice. But what we have learned already suggests that this would be a fruitful area of study. Future research in this area may help us to identify the foundational theories that competent teachers use in determining what they will do and how they will do it, within the educational enterprise. The theoretical foundations of professionalism in this field have been explored in this chapter, as has the conceptual mapping that will help us develop this area. As the details of the map are filled in, we will better understand the theoretical foundations of professional early childhood education practice.

REFERENCES

Apple, M. W., & King, N. R. (1977). What do teachers teach? *Curriculum Inquiry, 6,* 341–351.

Argyris, C., & Schön, D. A. (1975). *Theory-in-practice: Increasing professional effectiveness.* San Francisco: Jossey-Bass.

Berlak, A., Berlak, H., Bagantos, N. T., & Midel, E. P. (1975). Teaching and learning in the English primary schools. *School Review, 83,* 215–244.

Bernstein, B. (1975). *Class and pedagogies: Visible and invisible.* Paris: Organization for Economic Cooperation and Development.

Biber, B. (1984). *Early education and psychological development.* New Haven, CT: Yale University Press.

Bussis, A. M., Chittendon, E. A., & Amarel, M. (1976). *Beyond surface curriculum.* Boulder, CO: Westview Press.

Caldwell, B. (1984). From the president: Growth and development. *Young Children, 39*(6), 47–48.

Clark, C. M., & Peterson, P. L. (1986). Teachers' thought processes. In M. C. Wittrock (Ed.), *Handbook of research on teaching* (3rd ed.) (pp. 255–296). New York: Macmillan.

Clark, C. M., & Yinger, R. J. (1979). Teachers' thinking. In P. L. Peterson & H. J. Walberg (Eds.), *Research on teaching: Concepts, findings and implications.* Berkeley, CA: McCutchan.

Connelly, F. M. & Clandinin, D. J. (1984). Personal practical knowledge at Bay Street School. In R. Halkes & J. K. Olson (Eds.), *Teacher thinking: A new perspective.* Heirwig, Netherlands: Swets & Zeitlinger, pp. 134–148.

Elbaz, F. (1983). *Teacher thinking: A study of practical knowledge.* London: Croom Helm.

Halliwell, G. L. (1980). *Kindergarten teachers and curriculum construct systems.* Unpublished master's thesis, University of Illinois, Urbana-Champaign, IL.

Katz, L. G. (1984). The professional preschool teacher. In L. G. Katz (Ed.), *More talks with teachers* (pp. 27–42). Urbana, IL: ERIC Clearinghouse on Elementary and Early Childhood Education.

Kelly, G. A. (1955). *The psychology of personal constructs.* New York: W.W. Norton.

King, R. (1978). *All things bright and beautiful?* Chichester, England: John Wiley.

Spodek, B. (1987). Thought processes underlying preschool teachers' classroom decisions. *Early Child Care and Development, 28,* 197–208.

Spodek, B., & Rucinski, E. A. (1984, April). *A study of early childhood teachers' beliefs: Primary teachers.* Paper presented at the annual meeting of the American Educational Research Association, New Orleans, LA.

Spodek, B., & Rucinski, E. A. (1985). *A study of early childhood teachers' beliefs: Preschool teachers.* Paper presented at the annual meeting of the American Educational Research Association, Chicago, IL.

Yonemura, M. (1986). *A teacher at work: Professional development and the early childhood educator.* New York: Teachers College Press.

13 • Cognitive Style and Early Childhood Practice

OLIVIA N. SARACHO
University of Maryland

A great deal has been written about how teachers perform in the classroom and about how we can improve their performance. A focus on teachers' performance alone is inadequate, however. Teaching, like all professions, requires both performance skills and cognitive functioning. It is not enough for teachers to learn to act skillfully. They must also think about what they do, before, during, and after their actions, creating an intellectual basis for their performance. It is this intellectuality that creates the basis for professionalizing teaching and allows it to be modified on the basis of the information the teacher gathers in the process.

Our concern for professionalizing the field of early childhood education requires us to become more aware of these processes. Our understanding of teachers' cognitive functioning and the degree to which it can be modified may help to provide directions for increased professionalization as well as identify the limits of that potential.

Professionals, as a result of their training and experience, move beyond "doing what comes naturally" to functioning deliberately and rationally, in response to the demands of a profession. One element of cognitive functioning that has received a great deal of attention from educators and psychologists is cognitive style. This term connotes a consistent way in which individuals process information. One dimension of cognitive style that seems to relate to the way teachers and students perform in their classrooms is known as field-dependence-independence, which I will describe and discuss shortly. To date, this dimension has been the most extensively investigated and has had the widest application to educational concerns (Witkin, Dyk, Faterson, Goodenough, & Karp, 1962/1974; Witkin et al., 1954/1972). Although more research in this area needs to be conducted, there is reasonable evidence to suggest that knowledge of cognitive style may be applied to a number of educational issues. One of these issues, the cognitive styles of early childhood teachers, has implications for their professional development.

Teachers' cognitive styles interact with various elements in the classroom and affect educational practice, including "how students learn, how teachers teach, how teachers and students interact, and how students make their educational choices" (Witkin, Moore, Goodenough, & Cox, 1977, p. 2). The purpose of this chapter is to describe the field-dependence-independence dimension, to present studies that have examined the interactive effects of teachers' and students' field-dependent and field-independent cognitive styles, and to suggest ways of helping teachers improve their professional performance by adapting to the different cognitive styles of the children in their classroom.

THE FIELD-DEPENDENCE-INDEPENDENCE DIMENSION

Field-dependent and field-independent cognitive styles represent distinctly different methods of processing information. Field-independent individuals employ internal referents to guide them in processing information, whereas field-dependent individuals focus on external referents. Field-dependent and field-independent persons are differentiated by the techniques they use in dealing with complex and confusing events and in reacting cognitively to a variety of circumstances. Saracho compares and contrasts these behaviors by indicating the extremes of both cognitive styles. It should be noted that most individuals possess some of the characteristics of both field-dependence and field-independence, actually falling between these extremes. Saracho and Spodek (1981, p. 154) provide the following characteristics:

Field-dependent individuals:
rely on the surrounding perceptual field;
experience their environment in a relatively global fashion by conforming to the effects of the prevailing field or context;
depend on authority;
search for facial cues in those around them as a source of information;
are strongly interested in people;
get closer to the person with whom they are interacting;
have a sensitivity to others which helps them to acquire social skills;
prefer occupations which require involvement with others.

In contrast, field-independent individuals:
perceive objects as separate from the field;
can abstract an item from the surrounding field and solve problems that are presented and reorganized in different contexts;

experience an independence from authority which leads them to
depend on their own standards and values;
are oriented towards active striving;
appear to be cold and distant;
are socially detached but have analytic skills;
prefer occupations that allow them to work by themselves.

The individuals' behavior based on their cognitive style is extremely
consistent and long-lasting. In regard to teaching, field-dependent and
field-independent teachers select different teaching strategies, conduct
their classes differently, and exhibit different patterns of instructional
behavior, based on the predominance of their field-dependent or field-
independent characteristics. The following are descriptions of the two
types of teacher.

A Field-Dependent Teacher

Ms. Carlson is a kindergarten teacher. As a result of her scores on
the *Group Embedded Figures Test* (Witkin, Oltman, Raskin & Karp,
1971), *Articulation of the Body-Concept Scale* (Witkin, Dyk, Faterson,
Goodenough & Karp, 1962/1974), and the *Goodenough-Harris Drawing
Test* (Harris, 1963; Saracho, 1984, 1985, 1986), she has been characterized
as an extremely field-dependent person. Every morning Ms. Carlson
greets her students at the door with a smile, a hug, and a query about
their family affairs. For example, in greeting John, she hugs him and asks
him about his baby sister. She helps the children with their lunch boxes
and other personal belongings.

The first activity in Ms. Carlson's classroom is "sharing time," where
all children share their most important experience or object. She encourages all of the children to engage in conversation. Then they discuss the
activities in each learning center and her expectations of the children for
each activity. At this point, she gives the children important facts they
need to know. For instance, they will assume different roles in the dramatic play area, where a grocery store has been set up. She gives them
specific directions on the steps to follow when they enter the store, look
for the items they need, remove items from the shelf, look at the prices,
check their money, and pay the clerk.

The children play in activity centers for about an hour each morning.
During this time, Ms. Carlson circulates within the class and interacts
with the children. Just before quitting time, she places her hand on each
child's shoulder and informs him or her that the period is almost over.

Then she assembles the children in a circle and they discuss their experiences during the morning.

A Field-Independent Teacher

Ms. Gonzales is also a kindergarten teacher. Based on her scores on the same tests as Ms. Carlson took, she has been characterized as an extremely field-independent person. When children arrive in the classroom early in the morning, they place their personal belongings in the appropriate places and move their name tags on the magnetic board, to show they have arrived. Each learning center in the room is labeled and includes specific instructions for independent activities. At nine o'clock, Ms. Gonzales checks the magnetic board and records the names of the children who are present. As she rings a bell, the children take their places at the work tables. She then provides brief instructions about what is available at the learning centers. She tells them to watch the clock; when the little hand has moved to the next number (10), they must return to their chairs at the work tables.

The activities at the learning centers encourage problem solving. At the sand and water table, for example, children can measure sand and water in a variety of containers. There are also a number of different objects available near a water basin for children to use in determining which sink and which float. The children record their observations and check them against feedback from the teacher.

While the children are working, the teacher observes them and records their behavior in the different activities. At ten o'clock, she rings the bell and the children return to their places. Ms. Gonzales talks to them about their performance, correcting their mistakes. She believes that if children are told what they did wrong, children will learn from their mistakes and will not make them again.

Field-Dependence-Independence and Teaching Behaviors

Not only do professionals reflect their own dominant cognitive styles, but they also use different techniques in responding to the cognitive styles of their clients. For example, psychotherapists usually use more supportive methods for their field-dependent patients than for their field-independent patients (Greene, 1972; Karp, Kissin, & Hustmyer, 1970). They may also use quite different types of interpersonal relationships for field-dependent and field-independent patients. Karp et al. (1970) found similarities in the different treatments used for the two types of alcoholic patients. In their study, therapists tended to use insight psychotherapy for field-dependent patients and drug therapy for field-independent patients. Insight psychotherapy is a generally brief treatment in which the therapist encourages the patient to gain insight into her or his problem. On the other hand, drug therapy is an ongoing treatment in which the therapist prescribes to patients different types of drugs, especially tranquilizers and antidepressants.

Studies of the relationship of teachers' cognitive style to their teaching style have identified the cognitive and social features of both elements (Saracho, 1980, 1983b; Saracho & Dayton, 1980; Saracho & Spodek, 1981; Stone, 1976). In their teaching, field-dependent teachers tend to use a discussion approach, while field-independent teachers more often use a lecture approach.

Researchers have examined the classroom behavior of teachers with contrasting cognitive styles. While many of these studies are of teachers of older students, they do have implications for early childhood teachers. In a review of the literature, Witkin et al. (1977) found that field-dependent teachers preferred a warm and personal learning atmosphere and engaged their students in designing goals and directing their learning. In contrast, field-independent teachers attempted to focus on the intellectual elements of teaching rather than on the social elements. Wu's (1968) study showed that, in teaching social studies, more field-dependent student teachers preferred discussion to either lecture or discovery approaches, which were the preferences of more field-independent teachers. In teaching situations, apparently, field-dependent teachers prefer to interact personally with their students, while field-independent teachers prefer to be impersonal and focus on more abstract elements in their teaching.

Moore (1973) examined the differences in teachers' use of rules, relations, examples, and questions as they taught chemistry. The more field-independent teachers used questions to introduce topics and to respond to the students' answers, while the more field-dependent teachers used questions mainly to assess the students' learning after instruction.

Emmerich, Oltman, and McDonald (cited in Witkin et al., 1977) concluded that field-dependent teachers usually preferred class discussion over teacher lectures and more often preferred to involve the students in structuring the learning activity. Field-independent teachers used questioning more often than did field-dependent teachers in presenting new units and reacting to students' responses. The teachers' use of reinforcement was also related to their degree of field-dependence-independence. Field-independent teachers tended to use corrective feedback which showed students their mistakes and told them why they made a mistake. This was viewed as an efficient instructional method. The teachers were critical of their students, making negative judgments of them.

The studies by Jolly and Strawitz (1984) and Mahlios (1981) also suggest that the two types of teachers vary in the way they react to students who answer questions incorrectly. Mahlios found that field-independent teachers tend to employ corrective feedback to help students improve their learning performance, and they also tend to be more critical of those students who perform below their potential. He found that field-dependent teachers tend to ask more factual questions, while field-independent teachers tend to ask more analytic questions.

Emmerich and associates (cited in Witkin et al., 1977), like Mahlios (1981), showed that field-independent individuals had a major interest in abstract, theoretical, and structural issues, while field-dependent teachers were interested in teaching facts.

These studies demonstrate the relationship of teachers' field-dependence or field-independence to their teaching functions; however, the restricted nature of the variables explored and the sometimes conflicting results make generalization difficult.

The relationship between teacher style and student learning was studied by Stone (1976), who judged field-dependent teachers to be more suitable for teaching, especially in the lower grades. She found that these teachers provided more direct instruction, practice or review of skills and facts, and used more instructional materials. While the teachers' cognitive style was related to their method of instruction, it was not related to student performance. Field-independent second- and fifth-grade students came from higher socioeconomic backgrounds, their parents were better educated, and they had attended some preschool program other than Head Start. In contrast, field-dependent second- and fifth-grade students had lower socioeconomic backgrounds and had participated in Head Start, Title I, or a special reading program. The results may have been affected by the students' socioeconomic level, rather than by their cognitive style.

Ekstrom (1976) examined the teachers' style and its effects on students' learning and found that the teachers' style did not affect the students' learning. However, again, field-dependent teachers maintained more behavioral control in the classroom than field-independent teachers.

Saracho and Dayton (1980) found a relationship between teachers' cognitive styles and their students' standardized achievement test scores. Since students of field-independent teachers achieved higher scores on a standardized test than did students of field-dependent teachers, the authors concluded that field-independent teachers are probably more effective than field-dependent teachers. This outcome, however, may have been the result of teacher expectation creating a self-fulfilling prophecy (Rosenthal & Jacobson, 1968).

Saracho (1980) investigated the relation of second- and fifth-grade teachers' cognitive style to their perceptions of their students. Teachers were asked to rank their students according to their judgment of academic competence. Students were also ranked according to their scores on a standardized achievement test. In comparing the two rankings, field-independent teachers had more deviant and more positive scores for field-dependent students, whereas field-dependent teachers had more negative rankings for their field-independent students. Saracho's study indicates that field-independent teachers had higher expectations for students who differed from their cognitive style than did field-dependent teachers.

Since a significant number of studies have also shown a relationship between teachers' perceptions of their students, based on the teachers' and students' cognitive styles, Saracho and Spodek (1981) recommend that, for optimal academic success, assignments of students to teachers might be prioritized accordingly:

1. Field-independent students with field-independent teachers,
2. Field-dependent students with field-independent teachers,
3. Field-independent students with field-dependent teachers, and
4. Field-dependent students with field-dependent teachers.

While these recommendations differ from Packer and Bain's (1978), Frank and Davis (1982) suggest a similar placement. In a more recent study Jolly and Strawitz (1984) encountered the same pattern of results with a group of tenth-grade students as had Saracho and Spodek (1981). Although research shows that field-dependent teachers are better, the analysis in Saracho and Spodek's study showed that the number 1 match was most desirable, while the number 4 match was least desirable.

Using a different group of students (first- and third-graders), Saracho (1983b) examined the teachers' assessment of their students in relation to cognitive style. The results showed that both field-dependent and field-independent teachers underestimated both types of first-grade students; whereas field-dependent teachers overestimated both types of third-grade students. Field-independent teachers assessed their field-independent female students in close correlation to their scores on an achievement test.

In an earlier, similar study Saracho (1982) reported significant relationships among cognitive style, sex, and age:

1. Field-dependent teachers underestimated their field-dependent male and female students but underestimated their field-dependent male students more.
2. Field-dependent teachers overestimated their field-independent

female students and underestimated their field-independent male students more than their field-dependent male and female students.

3. Field-dependent teachers assessed their field-independent female students consistently with their test results.

4. Field-independent teachers underestimated their field-independent male students.

5. Field-independent teachers overestimated their field-dependent male students and underestimated their field-dependent female students.

More recently Saracho (1984) found a relationship between teachers' cognitive style and their characterization of their students in regard to attachment, indifference, concern, and rejection. Field-dependent teachers in general seemed more concerned about these aspects of their students than were the field-independent teachers.

The relationship of teachers' cognitive style to students' characteristics and learning style, as well as to instructional methods and curriculum content, has not been investigated to any great extent. There is some evidence to indicate, however, that field-dependent students usually learn better through a didactic instructional mode where rules and principles are explicitly stated rather than induced.

TEACHERS AND STUDENTS:
THE MATCHING AND MISMATCHING
OF COGNITIVE STYLES

Teachers and students can be matched in class assignments according to *identical matching style* or *performance matching style*. In identical matching style, teachers are matched with students who have the same cognitive style; thus they can explain and elaborate concepts in ways that are congruent with their students' way of thinking and problem solving. In *performance matching style*, students are assigned to teachers whose cognitive style it is believed will best promote their learning. When students and teachers are placed together in an educational setting, a variety of consequences can be predicted in relation to whether a student and a teacher are matched or mismatched in cognitive style.

Research studies contain few empirical results indicating the advantages and/or disadvantages of these different matching strategies. For a discussion of the complexities of the match/mismatch issues, see Miller (1981). Studies are equivocal; hence, Witkin et al. (1977) caution against making a priori decisions until more research evidence has been accumulated.

Identical Matching Style

Several studies on cognitive style provide a comparison between subjects assigned to dyads matched or mismatched in cognitive style. Most of the results suggest that matched persons perceive one another positively, whereas mismatched persons view one another negatively (DiStefano, 1970; Folman, 1973; Greene, 1972). The positive effects of identical matching style may be the result of common interests and personality features (Freedman, O'Hanlon, Oltman, & Witkin, 1972) and similar cognitive structures (Stasz, Shavelson, Cox, & Moore, 1976), which probably enhance good interpersonal relationships between dyad partners.

DiStefano (1970) studied extreme field-dependent and field-independent male teachers and students. Both teachers and students were asked to assess each other within six categories: evaluation, potency, activity, rationality, uniqueness, and sociability. The results showed that individuals who were identically matched in cognitive style usually described each other in positive terms, while teachers and students who were mismatched in cognitive style usually described each other in negative terms. DiStefano concludes that matched persons usually perceive each other more favorably.

Saracho (1984) examined the preferences of three-, four-, and five-year-old students for teachers matched or mismatched in cognitive style. In this study, the matched field-dependent teachers were the most preferred by the younger children.

Saracho (1984) investigated relationships between the teachers' cognitive style, matching, and categorizing of young students. The results showed that teachers categorized their matched three-, four-, and five-year-old students under *attachment* and their mismatched students under *rejection*. Cognitive style matching here seems preferable to cognitive style mismatching. In fact, all of the preceding studies suggest that a teacher-student match in cognitive style makes for greater interpersonal attraction than a mismatch.

Performance-Matching Style

Saracho (1984) investigated the significance of matching the cognitive style of three-, four-, and five-year-old students to their teachers. Her study showed that, for three-year-olds, though the teachers had a tendency to underestimate their matched students, they tended to underestimate their mismatched students even more. Although all teachers of four-year-old students tended to overestimate their students in both groups, they estimated their mismatched students higher. For five-year-olds, field-dependent teachers perceived their matched students more negatively than did field-independent teachers, while field-independent teachers perceived their mismatched students more positively than field-dependent teachers.

Saracho (1983b) also found that both field-dependent and field-independent first-grade teachers usually underestimated their matched and mismatched students, while field-dependent third-grade teachers usually overestimated their mismatched students and field-independent third-grade teachers usually assessed their matched students similarly to their outcomes on a standardized test. She also found a relationship between field-dependence-independence and the teachers' perceptions of their matched and mismatched students, related to sex. While field-dependent teachers underestimated both their matched male and female students, they underestimated their female students more. In relation to the mismatch, field-dependent teachers overestimated their female students but underestimated their male students more than both their matched male and female students.

In comparison, field-independent teachers assessed their matched female students similarly to a standardized achievement test but underestimated their matched male students in relation to that test. Mismatched field-independent teachers overestimated their male students and underestimated their female students.

The match and mismatch of field-dependent and field-independent cognitive styles and the students' perceptions of an ideal teacher were examined by Coward, Davis, & Wichern (1978), who found that field-independent students did not favor teachers with more socially oriented characteristics. Saracho and Dayton (1980) found that students with field-independent teachers, regardless of whether matched or mismatched, showed greater gains in achievement scores than students with field-dependent teachers. Significant effects were found on gains in academic achievement related to teachers' cognitive styles, but there was no significant main or interaction effect associated with either matching or grade level.

Saracho (1980) found that the teachers' cognitive styles may relate significantly to student expectations. Field-independent teachers had higher expectations for students with mismatched cognitive style than did field-dependent teachers. Saracho and Spodek (1981) also found that both field-independent and field-dependent students achieved better test scores with field-independent teachers. Thus, it may be best to match students according to their performance style rather than their cognitive style. It may be that in a mismatch situation the field-dependent individual benefits from some of the skills of the field-independent individual. Coward et al. (1978) suggested that the significance of such a mismatch may be that the field-dependent individuals are aware of or have a need for certain characteristics which can compensate for their own weaknesses. They found that field-dependent students showed more of a preference than did field-independent students for teacher characteristics reflecting field-independent cognitive style.

The performance-matching style must not be interpreted to mean that opposite characteristics attract, that is, that students prefer someone with characteristics they lack. Despite the students' social orientation that was greater than their teachers', Coward et al. (1978) demonstrated that students, regardless of their own personal cognitive orientations, preferred teachers who possessed positive social characteristics.

It may be that teachers and students will function better under both identical-matching style or performance-matching style conditions; however, evidence from the cited studies demonstrates that the matching relationship is not a straightforward one.

We need to understand more about the characteristics and abilities that distinguish field-dependent and field-independent individuals and the consequences of various ways of matching students and teachers based on their styles. Becoming sensitive to the educational implications of the different cognitive styles can improve the relationship between the teachers and students (Doebler & Eicke, 1979). Knowledge of cognitive style can assist teachers in making such decisions as whether or not it is appropriate at certain times to encourage a field-independent cognitive style, or if perhaps it is best to encourage an awareness of both cognitive styles, along with teaching strategies that capitalize on the characteristics of each.

TEACHERS' COGNITIVE FLEXIBILITY AS A BASIS FOR PROFESSIONALIZING BEHAVIOR

The studies reviewed in the last sections indicate that, based on prior knowledge of cognitive style, the matching of cognitive style and performance style can have a significant impact on the education of young children; however, the evidence on how this occurs is not clear.

Although there is no supporting evidence, early childhood educators often suggest that persons who possess warmth, nurturance, and social skills are better teachers of younger children. These are the characteristics of a field-dependent person. At least in relation to academic achievement, the research suggests that field-independent teachers, even of young children, are probably more effective. Since field-dependent individuals tend to be strongly interested in others and in social affairs, field-dependent teachers may focus on social goals in the classroom. On the other hand, field-independent individuals, who tend to be more socially detached, impersonal, and oriented toward striving, may emphasize cognitive achievement in the classroom.

Research on teacher expectation suggests that teachers' expectations of academic success affect their students' actual success. Since teachers' perceptions vary in relation to the match or mismatch of cognitive styles, successful matching can improve the academic status of students by creating an expectation for academic success.

If teachers' behaviors related to cognitive style do indeed affect young students' learning, then it is essential that cognitive style characteristics be considered in selecting or preparing teachers. Field-dependent teachers might be selected when social goals are given priority, while field-independent teachers might be selected when academic goals are given priority. In order to support integrated social and academic goals, teachers may be trained to achieve "cognitive flexibility" (Saracho & Spodek, 1986). This would suggest that, for teachers to function in a more professional manner, they should be responsive to the cognitive styles of their students rather than to their own, much like the psychotherapists noted earlier. To achieve this cognitive flexibility, a person's cognitive style can be identified and then modified to help her or him use both field-dependent and field-independent characteristics. Support for the value of cognitive flexibility is provided by Saracho (1983a).

The modification of teachers' cognitive style is an important concern, since different styles may facilitate or stifle students' learning. One cognitive style can be maladaptive in one specific instructional context while it may be of benefit elsewhere. Saracho and Spodek (1986) provide the following example:

> A teacher may plan a mathematics activity, which is considered a field-independent activity, with a field-dependent child. This child may encounter difficulty with formal instruction in mathematics but can probably learn the concept better through dramatic play, which is a social activity. To help this child learn mathematics in an abstract mode, his/her cognitive style needs to be modified to adequately function in a field-independent mode. In contrast, field-independent individuals can easily perform cognitive problem-solving tasks but may not be able to perform tasks requiring social sensitivity, interpersonal harmony and other important affective characteristics. [p. 181]

Both adults and children have demonstrated the ability to use both field-dependent and field-independent cognitive styles, displaying what

Ramírez and Castañeda (1974) refer to as "bicognitive development." In different situations, persons tend to cooperate or compete, solve problems through inductive or deductive reasoning, and respond to or ignore the social atmosphere. Individuals need to obtain a repertoire of field-dependent and field-independent strategies which can be utilized in the process of learning and solving a problem.

Individuals can learn to extend their repertoire beyond those techniques related to their dominant cognitive style (Ramírez & Castañeda, 1974). Teachers can be provided with experiences that match their dominant cognitive style until they feel comfortable and secure with it. They can then be gradually presented with experiences that do not match their dominant cognitive style. A degree of "cognitive dissonance" can guide teachers in making the transition and being able to interchange one cognitive style with the other (Saracho & Spodek, 1981). Field-independent teachers can engage in experiences such as chairing a committee, working with a group on a school project, or joining with others in selecting equipment and material for the classroom. Such experiences demand that they use their social sensitivity, a field-dependent characteristic. Conversely, field-dependent teachers can engage in experiences requiring them to use their analytic skills, a field-independent characteristic. Examples include working alone in solving a problem relating to writing their curriculum or lesson plans, designing their classroom environment, or creating a mathematics task.

This process can assist teachers to react more professionally in their interactions with their students. While Ramírez and Castañeda (1974) and Saracho and Spodek (1981, 1986) have found that individuals are able to learn to perform in a different cognitive style from their dominant one, it must be noted that this apparently modifies the individuals' traits but does not wholly change them. Additional developmentally oriented research needs to be conducted on the cognitive flexibility and bicognitive development of persons from different groups, ages, and sexes, as well as on the impact of such modification on the professional development of teachers.

REFERENCES

Coward, R. T., David, J. K., & Wichern, R. O. (1978). Cognitive style and perceptions of the ideal teacher. *Contemporary Educational Psychology, 3,* 232–238.

DiStefano, J. J. (1970). Interpersonal perceptions of field independent and field dependent teachers and students (Doctoral dissertation, Cornell University, 1969). *Dissertation Abstracts International, 31,* 463A–464A.

Doebler, L. K., & Eicke, F. J. (1979). Effects of teacher awareness of the educational implications of field-dependent/field-independent cognitive style on selected classroom variables. *Journal of Educational Psychology, 71,* 226–232.

Ekstrom, R. B. (1976). Teacher aptitudes, knowledge, attitudes and cognitive style as predictors of teacher behavior. *Journal of Teacher Education, 27,* 329–331.

Folman, R. Z. (1973). Therapist-patient perceptual style, interpersonal attraction, initial interview behavior, and premature termination (Doctoral dissertation, Boston University, 1973). *Dissertation Abstracts International, 34,* 1746B. (University Microfilms No. 73–23, 482)

Frank, B. M., & Davis, J. K. (1982). Effect of field-independence match or mismatch on a communication task. *Journal of Educational Psychology, 74,* 23–31.

Freedman, N., O'Hanlon, J., Oltman, P., & Witkin, H. A. (1972). The imprint of psychological differentiation on kinetic behavior in varying communicative contexts. *Journal of Abnormal Psychology, 79,* 239–258.

Greene, M. A. (1972). Client perception of the relationship as a function of worker-client cognitive styles (Doctoral dissertation, Columbia University, 1972). *Dissertation Abstracts International, 33,* 3030A–3031A. (University Microfilms No. 72–31, 213)

Harris, D. B. (1963). *Children's drawings as measures of intellectual maturity.* New York: Harcourt Brace Jovanovich.

Jolly, P.E., & Strawitz, B.M. (1984). Teacher-student cognitive style and achievement in biology. *Science Education, 68,* 485–490.

Karp, S. A., Kissin, B., & Hustmyer, F. E. (1970). Field dependence as a predictor of alcoholic therapy dropouts. *Journal of Nervous and Mental Disease, 150,* 77–83.

Mahlios, M.C. (1981). Instructional design and cognitive styles of teachers in elementary schools. *Perceptual and Motor Skills, 52,* 335–338.

Miller, A. (1981). Conceptual matching models and interactional research in education. *Review of Educational Research, 51*(1), 33–84.

Moore, C. A. (1973). Styles of teacher behavior under simulated teaching conditions (Doctoral dissertation, Stanford University, Stanford, CA, 1973). *Dissertation Abstracts International, 34,* 3149A–3150A. (University Microfilms No. 73–30, 449)

Packer, J., & Bain, J. D. (1978). Cognitive style and teacher-student compatibility. *Journal of Educational Psychology, 70,* 864–871.

Ramírez, M. III, & Castañeda, A. (1974). *Cultural democracy, bicognitive development, and education.* New York: Academic Press.

Ross, H. G. (1980). Matching achievement styles and instructional environments. *Contemporary Educational Psychology, 5,* 216–226.

Saracho, O. N. (1980). The relationship between teachers' cognitive styles and their perceptions of their students' academic achievement. *Educational Research Quarterly, 5*(3), 40–49.

Saracho, O. N. (1982, March). *The cognitive style of teachers and their perceptions* of their matched and mismatched children's academic competence. Paper presented at the annual meeting of the American Educational Research Association, New York, NY.

Saracho, O. N. (1983a). Cultural differences in the cognitive style of Mexican American students. *Journal of the Association for the Study of Perception, 18*(1), 3–10.

Saracho, O. N. (1983b). Relationship between cognitive style and teachers' perceptions of young children's academic competence. *The Journal of Experimental Education, 51*(4), 184–189.

Saracho, O. N. (1984, April). *Educational implications of matched and mismatched students' and teachers' cognitive styles.* Paper presented at the annual conference of the American Educational Research Association, New Orleans, LA.

Saracho, O. N. (1984). The Goodenough-Harris Drawing Test as a measure of field-dependence-independence. *Perceptual and Motor Skills, 59,* 887–892.

Saracho, O. N. (1985). A modification in scoring the ABC Scale. *Journal of Personality Assessment, 49,* 154–155.

Saracho, O. N. (1986). Validation of two cognitive measures to assess field-dependence-independence. *Perceptual and Motor Skills, 63,* 255–263.

Saracho, O. N., & Dayton, C. M. (1980). Relationship of teachers' cognitive styles to pupils' academic achievement gains. *Journal of Educational Psychology, 72,* 544–547.

Saracho, O. N., & Spodek, B. (1981). Teachers' cognitive styles and their educational implications. *Educational Forum, 45,* 153–159.

Saracho, O. N., & Spodek, B. (1986). Cognitive style and children's learning: Individual variation in cognitive processes. In L. G. Katz (Ed.), *Current topics in early childhood education* (Vol. 11) (pp. 177–194). Norwood, NJ: Ablex.

Stasz, C., Shavelson, R. J., Cox, D. L., & Moore, C. A. (1976). Field independence and the structuring of knowledge in a social studies minicourse. *Journal of Educational Psychology, 68,* 550–558.

Stone, M. K. (1976). The role of cognitive style in teaching and learning. *Journal of Teacher Education, 27,* 332–334.

Witkin, H. A. (1974). Cognitive style perspective on evaluation and guidance. In *Proceedings of the 1973 Invitational Conference on Testing Problems—Measurement for self-understanding and personal development* (pp. 21–27). Princeton, NJ: Educational Testing Service.

Witkin, H. A., Dyk, R. B., Faterson, H. F., Goodenough, D. R., & Karp, S. A. (1974). *Psychological differentiation.* Potomac, MD: Lawrence Erlbaum Associates. (Original work published 1962)

Witkin, H. A., Lewis, H. B., Hertzman, M., Machover, K., Meissner, P. B., & Wapner, S. (1972). *Personality through perception.* Westport, CT: Greenwood Press. (Original work published 1954)

Witkin, H. A., Moore, C. A., Goodenough, D. R., & Cox, P. W. (1977). Field-dependent and field-independent cognitive styles and their educational implications. *Review of Educational Research, 47*(1), 1–64.

Witkin, H. A., Oltman, P. K., Raskin, E., & Karp, S. A. (1971). *Group Embedded Figures Test*. Palo Alto, CA: Consulting Psychologists Press.

Wu, J. J. (1968). Cognitive style and task performance: A study of student teachers (Doctoral dissertation, University of Minnesota, 1967). *Dissertation Abstracts International, 29*, 176A. (University Microfilms No. 67–7408)

14 • Professionalizing the Field: The Tasks Ahead

BERNARD SPODEK
University of Illinois

OLIVIA N. SARACHO
University of Maryland

DONALD L. PETERS
University of Delaware

The concern for professionalizing practice evolved as the field of early childhood education has emerged over the last 150 years in the United States. Changes in the structure and purposes of the field as well as changes involving the populations served have all had their influence.

THE ROOTS OF PROFESSIONALISM

The call for professionalization first came in the field of kindergarten education. Later nursery school education was added, along with child care, preprimary education, early intervention, and early primary education. With each new addition there were new concerns, new purposes, new understandings, and new skills needed and new demands for professionalizing practice. For example, kindergarten teachers, in the early days of the field, were not expected to have an understanding of the developmental patterns of children. Rather, they needed to be immersed in the philosophy of Freidrich Froebel and in the uses of the *gifts* and *occupations* that he had designed. A kindergarten teacher who had studied in a particular institution or trained under a known kindergarten educator was considered competent. There were few enough kindergartens that each practitioner's lineage could be easily traced and each person's abilities were common knowledge.

When nursery schools were introduced to the field and kindergartens transformed by the progressive education philosophy, knowledge of Froebel's philosophy and methodology became, in the minds of some, obsolete and even irrelevant. The emphasis was placed on attaining a working level of knowledge in child development and learning. Fed by the growing child-study movement, this knowledge became expected of early childhood teachers. Later, teachers employed in child-care institutions, where they became responsible for nurturing a greater portion of the life of the child, had additional expectations placed upon them, including knowledge of child nutrition and childhood diseases.

Changes in expectations for early childhood practitioners were also influenced by changes in the sponsorship and funding of early childhood educational services. The first early childhood programs were privately owned, with the owners deeply involved in their operation, or they were associated with philanthropic institutions committed to serving needy children. Such individuals and institutions were accountable to themselves only or to their lay boards. There was little sense of accountability, either to the client or to the larger society. Since there were no public funds involved, there was no need for public accountability.

As colleges, universities, and especially public schools became involved, early childhood education moved away from being an individual enterprise and became part of a larger and more bureaucratic system. There was less of a face-to-face quality to the relationship between the early childhood practitioner and both parents and sponsors. As early childhood programs became more commonly available and more institutionalized, the determination of competence became less reliant on educational lineage and more reliant on "objectified" assessments of knowledge and skill. Concerns for qualified practitioners were translated into concerns for the certification or credentialiing of practitioners and the accreditation of early childhood teacher preparation programs.

More recently, the field of early childhood education became democratized, with large numbers of young children from different backgrounds enrolled in a wide array of nearly universally available programs, taught by large numbers of practitioners, diverse in background and preparation. With this expansion, there came an increased need to establish publicly verifiable criteria for those entering and practicing in the field. These criteria, in addition to being more easily communicated to the public, presumably would insure that those practitioners with the appropriate credentials were competent to provide developmentally appropriate programs to serve children's needs. Competence here, as in other fields, was tied to objective qualifications, since it was too difficult for everyone concerned to make an independent judgment of competence. Thus, as in other fields moving toward professionalization, educational qualifications or "paper" credentials were seen as needed for entry into the field.

PRESENT CONCERNS ABOUT PROFESSIONALISM

Currently there are a number of concerns related to professionalism that have been raised in the field of early childhood education. The most important are contained in the following seven questions.

How do we establish standards of quality for practitioners in the field? Is there a core of knowledge, skills, understandings, and values that all practitioners in the field use, regardless of the agency for which they work, the type of service they provide, or the age level and developmental stage of the children they serve? Standards are established in professional fields by creating a form of license to practice. Currently, there are different standards within early childhood education for those who serve the youngest than for those who serve older children. Haberman describes in Chapter 7 of this book the break between the teachers of children under five and those who teach children five through eight. This break is determined to a great extent by the fact that the younger children are not enrolled in public schools, while the older ones are. Thus, teachers of the older children, because of their affiliation with the public schools, must meet teacher certification requirements imposed by one part of the state bureaucracy, while teachers of the youngest children, because of their affiliation with day care or early intervention programs such as Head Start, have fewer, if any, requirements imposed on them.

If the field of early childhood education is concerned with insuring that all children are properly served, whether they are in kindergartens, primary classes, child-care centers, or other institutions, then there must be some way of establishing and implementing standards for practitioners. But we still need to determine if the same standards are reasonable for all practitioners. We need to be concerned with establishing a definition of competent practice and the criteria needed to meet it, to insure that early childhood practitioners serve all children well. Generic criteria of competence may not be feasible. If they are not, then the issue of specialization within the field of early childhood education will have to be addressed.

What standards of early childhood professionalism are reasonable in our field? Aside from the issue of general versus specialized practice, we must question whether there is a single standard for the level of professionalism that can be applied to all practitioners in the field. Rather than seeking a single concept for the term *professional,* we might better identify various levels of professionalism. This approach is taken by the National Association for the Education of Young Children's standards of professionalism. It is also implied in the developmental levels of professionalism that can be reached by practitioners as presented by Vander Ven in Chapter 11. She suggests that levels of accomplishment exist that relate to stages in an early childhood practitioner's career.

How should entry to the field be determined? At present the determination of standards for early childhood teachers is in the hands of at least two agencies in each state. Although they vary in name across states, they are usually identifiable as an education agency and a social welfare agency. Teacher certification standards are established by an education agency to insure minimal qualifications of teachers in public and sometimes in private schools. Day-care licensing standards, established by a social welfare agency, include qualifications for practitioners, often differentiated by level of responsibility. The Child Development Associate credential is accepted by many day-care licensing agencies as well as by Head Start programs as certifying competency. Hence, though they use somewhat different mechanisms, the two forms of licensure serve the same function.

The standards of these two forms are different from one another, with public school teacher certification requiring more preservice preparation within a four-year college or university program. We need to determine if we have inappropriately established levels of licensure that are unequal and, if this is the case, whether the differences created best serve the needs of children, their families, the profession, and the public. We also need to address very seriously whether a two-tiered system perpetuates socioeconomic, racial, and ethnic divisions in society.

To complicate matters further, there is presently a scheme developing to establish a new national teacher credential. It is still not clear how this will impact on the field of early childhood education.

Should the field of early childhood education become more inclusive or more exclusive? Often the strength of the field of early childhood education has been related to its inclusivity. Many people with different backgrounds and different preparations serve the field. This has allowed a wealth of resources from many disciplines—such as anthropology, social work, psychology and sociology—to be brought to bear on the field. It has also allowed individuals from different cultures and different backgrounds, many of whom have been denied access to higher education, to become upwardly mobile by becoming early childhood practitioners. By requiring higher levels of preparation and establishing standards for entry to practice, we might establish a standard of more competent practice while simultaneously denying some individuals the opportunity to become early childhood practitioners. We need to find ways of balancing what may be competing values.

How should standards be applied, and by whom?　At present standards for practitioners are established and implemented by a variety of state agencies, as just noted. While the field, through the National Association for the Education of Young Children, has been able to influence standards for early childhood teacher education programs, it has not influenced certification standards. Though the association currently sponsors the CDA, those credentialing standards are not necessarily the standards that are required by each state. If we are to achieve a level of professionalism, we will need to find ways of influencing state agencies in establishing standards that are approved by the members of the profession themselves. We also need to influence the public at large regarding the importance of high-quality early education programs staffed by competent, professional practitioners.

How should gender and economic issues be dealt with? There are many issues within the larger society that influence the establishment of professional standards in our field, and some may be beyond our ability to control. Two of these are the gender and the economics issues. In many ways they are intertwined.

Early childhood education has traditionally been a women's field. Even today, men make up a small proportion of the practitioners within it. The career patterns of men and women also suggest that men are more likely than women to have upwardly mobile careers, moving more quickly from positions as classroom practitioners to supervisors, administrators, and teacher educators. Like other traditionally female fields, salaries are lower than in other occupations that require comparable preparation.

The economic base of early childhood education also limits the salaries of practitioners. In most cases, parents directly pay the fees for early childhood services for children below school age. This places limits on the costs that can be charged for such services and, therefore, on the salaries that are paid to practitioners involved in offering the services.

Both of these elements influence the decisions of those who enter the field and may lead them to leave prematurely, not because of psychological burnout but as a way of escaping poverty. To attempt to establish standards of professionalism without addressing the issue of professional compensation is to deal with issues of professionalism in an unrealistic way.

How do we define professional knowledge and values? There are knowledge issues that must be addressed in relation to developing professionalism in early childhood education. To establish professional standards is to assert that there is a body of knowledge, skills, and values that must be shared by all those who practice. Studies of teachers in action suggest not only that it is important for teachers to have a repertoire of behavioral skills and a set of principles upon which to base actions, but that the way in which teachers think about that practice may be equally important. The professional act is not simply a set of observable performances; the way teachers function in a professional situation is related to how they think about that situation. We must deal with basic cognitive processes related to problem solving and decision making within the realm of early childhood educational practice.

We must also deal with how people feel about what they do: what they consider to be right for children, as well as what they consider to be true. The call for codes of ethics for early childhood educators underlines this important concern. There is a set of values that separates competent practitioners—professionals—from laypersons. These values can form a code of ethics.

Finally, we must realize that a move toward increased professionalization of the field will have its costs as well as its benefits. There may be increasing distance placed between practitioners and parents. There may also be hurdles created for those becoming early childhood practitioners that will place limits on those intent on entering the field. All these must be considered in the debate that will be conducted prior to any action the field takes related to the professional status of early childhood practitioners.

About the Editors
and the Contributors

Millie Almy is Professor Emerita at the University of California, Berkeley. Her long career includes teaching young children, case work in a rural children's agency, directing nursery schools and child care centers, as well as teaching developmental psychology and early education. Previously, she held professorial appointments at the University of Cincinnati and at Teachers College, Columbia University. She is the author of many articles and books, including *Child Development, Ways of Studying Children, Young Children's Thinking,* and *The Early Childhood Educator at Work.*

Barbara Biber has worked to integrate the insights of developmental psychology with educational practice and ideology, for more than fifty years. In her association with Bank Street College of Education she has served as an instructor, established a research program, and developed an active program of advisement for individual students. In the 1940s and 1950s she helped establish teacher workshops in New York City public schools and served in the 1960s as a member of the National Commission on the Mental Health of Children. She helped establish principles that became the foundation for federally funded day care and Head Start programs in the 1970s. Her most recent book is *Early Education and Psychological Development.*

Barbara Finkelstein is Professor of Education Policy and Director of the Center for the Study of Education Policy and Human Values, Department of Education Policy, University of Maryland, College Park. She is an historian and critic of education, who has written extensively on the evolution of childhood, the family, and the role of teachers in American history. Her latest book, *Governing the Young: Teacher Behavior in Popular Primary Schools in the United States in the Nineteenth Century,* is forthcoming.

Martin Haberman is Professor of Education, University of Wisconsin-Milwaukee. He has played a significant role in the shaping of major developments in teacher education: MAT programs, the original NCATE standards, the National Teacher Corps, the Training of Teacher Trainers

(TTT) program, NDEA Institutes, Professional Development Centers, Alternative Certification programs, and, currently, a range of pre- and inservice programs.

Lilian G. Katz is Professor of Early Childhood Education and Director of the ERIC Clearinghouse on Elementary and Early Childhood Education at the University of Illinois, Urbana-Champaign. Her interest in preschool education developed from experience as a participating mother in parent cooperative nursery schools. She is Editor-in-Chief of the *Early Childhood Research Quarterly* of the National Association for the Education of Young Children.

Donald L. Peters (editor), who received his Ph.D. in Educational Psychology from Stanford University, is currently Professor and Chair, Department of Individual and Family Studies, University of Delaware. From 1968–1985 he was at the Pennsylvania State University, and has done research and evaluation work with Head Start, day care, and early intervention programs for handicapped children and their families since 1966. He is the author of some 60 articles and several books in the field of early childhood education.

Olivia N. Saracho (editor) is Associate Professor at the University of Maryland. She received her Ph.D. in early childhood education from the University of Illinois in 1978. Prior to that, she taught Head Start, preschool, kindergarten, and elementary classes in Brownsville, Texas, and was Director of the Child Development Associate Program at Pan American University. Her current research and writing are in the areas of cognitive style, academic learning, and teacher education in relation to early childhood education. Dr. Saracho is the co-author of *Foundations of Early Childhood Education*.

Kelvin Seifert received his Ph.D. in psychology and education from the University of Michigan in 1973. Both before and after that, he taught nursery- and kindergarten-age children for several years. Currently, he is Professor of Educational Psychology at the University of Manitoba, Canada, where he is coordinator of early childhood teacher training. Dr. Seifert has published articles about gender influences on early childhood education as a career, and is the author of *Educational Psychology*, and co-author of *Child and Adolescent Development*.

Jonathan G. Silin was an early childhood teacher for ten years before receiving an Ed.D. from Teachers College, Columbia University. He has taught at Bank Street College of Education, Long Island University, and Colgate University. His research interests include the role of men in early education, the nature of pedagogical authority, and the meaning of professionalism. Currently, he is Director of Education at the Long Island Association for AIDS Care, where he has helped many schools develop AIDS-education curricula and policies. His most recent publication, "The Language of AIDS: Public Fears, Pedagogical Responsibilities," appeared in the *Teachers College Record* (Fall, 1987).

Bernard Spodek (editor) has been Professor of Early Childhood Education at the University of Illinois since 1965. He received his Ed.D. from Teachers College, Columbia University and he has taught nursery, kindergarten, and elementary school. His research and scholarly interests are in the areas of curriculum, teaching, and teacher education in early childhood education. Dr. Spodek has lectured extensively in the United States, Australia, Canada, China, Israel, Japan, Mexico, and Taiwan. From 1976–78 he was President of the National Association for the Education of Young Children, and from 1981–83 he chaired the Early Education and Child Development Special Interest Group of the American Educational Research Association. He is widely published in the field of early childhood education; his most recent books are *Today's Kindergarten* and *Foundations of Early Childhood Education.*

Karen Vander Ven, Ph.D., is Professor of Child Development and Child Care in the Program in Child Development and Child Care, School of Social Work, University of Pittsburgh. Previously she worked with children of all ages and parents in a variety of settings, including several laboratory preschools. She has published in the areas of career paths in early childhood education and child care, professionalization of child care, and work with parents. Dr. Vander Ven is Associate Editor of the *Child Care Quarterly* and of *Children in Contemporary Society*, and was recently elected to membership in the International Federation of Educative Communities and to the Academy of Child and Youth Care Professionals.

· Index